History of Italy

*A Captivating Guide to Italian History,
Starting from the First Settlements through
the Middle Ages to the Modern Period*

Free Bonus from Captivating History
(Available for a Limited time)

Hi History Lovers!

Now you have a chance to join our exclusive history list so you can get your first history ebook for free as well as discounts and a potential to get more history books for free! Simply visit the link below to join.

Captivatinghistory.com/ebook

Also, make sure to follow us on Facebook, Twitter and Youtube by searching for Captivating History.

Contents

Introduction

It is not an easy job to draw the border between the history of Italy and the history of Rome. In so many places, the two political and geographical entities collide. They wouldn't be possible without each other, but they each have their own story. Rome's history is only a small fragment of Italy's history. Although it is just a city, Rome was the birthplace of the republic, a great empire, and notable philosophers, poets, and artists. But on a larger scale, Rome expanded its borders, spreading not only through Italy but also through the whole known world. In that context, Rome ceased being only a city; it also became a universal imperial symbol and the pride of Italy.

Italy wasn't a united nation until the 19th century, which means the history of this country is very fragmented. It is the job of historians, archaeologists, anthropologists, linguists, and various scientists to pick up the pieces of the peninsula's past and put them together. Only then will we have a clear picture, a mosaic if you will, of the past of one of the most significant nations of Europe and the world. And after it is pieced together, we need to deconstruct the mosaic and take a look at each fragment to learn about the different peoples, cultures, and religions that were and still are a part of Italy.

The Roman Empire is constantly talked about in various books, plays, movies, and art. They teach us about the greater and lesser emperors of Italy, but barely anyone asks themselves what the rest of Italy was like. The Roman Empire might have united the geographical region of Italy on a political level, but it failed to unite its people. The emperors detested the idea of a unified nation, as they saw it as a threat to their rule. Instead, they treated the people outside of Rome proper as foreigners, as subjects who should honor their great and wise Roman leaders, even if they lived in Italy. While imperial Rome had all the advantages of citizenship, the rest of Italy was excluded. In the beginning, people couldn't vote, marry, own property, inherit the property from their fathers, be priests, or even enlist in the legions. However, when the need for people and resources arose during Rome's foreign wars, Rome opened itself to all Italians.

When Rome finally fell due to the barbarian invasions, the people were again divided. Each region had to fight its own enemy, and each city had its own ruler. But the people adapted and learned how to survive the darkness of the Middle Ages. Constant invasions, wars, and various territorial conflicts weakened Italy, but its people started dreaming of unification. However, it was still a far-off dream. The Renaissance and humanism brought new competition. This time, it wasn't with a foreign ruler; rather, the cities fought between themselves for trade and cultural supremacy. This wasn't only a physical conflict on the battlefield, as it was also led behind the closed doors of diplomats, religious leaders, philosophers, engineers, bankers, and artists.

Many wealthy families emerged as leaders of their cities, communes, or republics. But they soon displayed the wish for a monarchic rule. Their wealth and prosperity were only an invitation for new foreign invaders, and the French, Spanish, and Austrians started fighting for supremacy on the Italian Peninsula.

Italy would remain the battlefield where various foreign powers would play until the end of the Napoleonic Wars. They left Italy in ruins, but the people finally realized that unification was necessary. It was then or never. They couldn't allow themselves to be divided and governed by others anymore, and they finally rose in rebellion. It took three wars to finally unify Italy into a single nation. The Kingdom of Italy was finally born, with Victor Emmanuel II as the first king. Unfortunately, this king's grandson would lead Italy into the disasters of the First World War, Mussolini's fascist regime, and finally into the Second World War. These conflicts once more brought Italy down to its knees, and the country was destroyed, torn apart not only by war but also by internal political conflicts. It was time for the people to again say "No more!" The proud people of Italy voted for the republic in 1946, leading their country into a better tomorrow and transforming it into what Italy is today. It is now a land where history meets innovation and where various religions and peoples live in peace and unity.

Chapter 1 – The Bronze Age in Italy and the Early Settlements

Italy has always been a diverse land. To this day, it is inhabited by migrants from all over the world, and being Italian might mean one has roots in Spain or Albania. This can even be seen in some Italian family names, such as Spagnuolo, Greco, or Albano. But the diversity of Italy can be best observed if we look at its prehistory. Before the rise of Rome and its conquest of the rest of the peninsula, Italy was a patchwork of various peoples, cultures, and tribes. This part of Europe had been inhabited since the early Paleolithic period, and it had always attracted migratory tribes. This is because Italy lies in a perfect geographical location, as it is where the paths from the whole Mediterranean world meet. It also connects Europe north of the Alps with the sea routes to the Far East. These routes were essential for trade throughout history.

In prehistory, probably the most important role of Italy was that it linked Europe with the Mediterranean world. Because of this diversity and Italy's importance, the prehistory of the region is essential to the prehistory of the whole world. The Po Valley is easily accessible through the mountain passes of the north, and from there, the northern Adriatic Sea is at Europe's disposal. Ships could take people and their goods to Mediterranean destinations. However, it was the migration of people, not trade, that marked Italy's early prehistory. The archaeological evidence of various pottery originated in the Po Valley, but they found their way to the shores of the Atlantic Ocean. The same pottery evidence was found in the archaeological sites of France and Portugal, and it suggests a large migration of peoples from the Mediterranean to the west.

Unfortunately, there is little evidence that could give us more insight into the early prehistory of Italy. While archaeological findings exist, they are too few to bring forth any decisive conclusions. The dawn of history lacks written evidence, so only artifacts can provide information about the remote past. But pottery, early copper tools, crude stone statues, and urns can only tell historians so much; there is so much more that remains hidden from us. Nevertheless, scholars agree that a decisive point of the cultural development of Italy was during the Bronze Age (2300-950 BCE). During this period, people mostly settled in the mountainous regions of Italy's north, as well as the fertile plains of today's Venice. This region, in particular, looked completely different geographically from what we know today. The sea level of the Adriatic Sea was much lower, and what is today under water used to be a fertile valley with many lakes. The Po Valley is famous for its early terramare settlements, where some of the houses were built on poles, even though this area is not known to be wet. Perhaps in the past, it was, but no evidence would provide such a conclusion.

Early Bronze Age (c. 2300-1700 BCE)

With the beginning of the Early Bronze Age, which started around 2300 BCE, a new cultural cycle in Italy started: the Polada culture. It is believed that the Polada culture had its roots in the previous Bell Beaker culture of the Iberian Peninsula, but it also shows strong links to central Europe. Its occurrence corresponds with the movement of the peoples from Germany and Switzerland to northern Italy. In fact, even though Italy is a Mediterranean country, it would always be culturally closer to Europe than the rest of the Mediterranean world. The Polada culture's settlements were predominantly concentrated around the wet areas of the Alpine region. The villages were erected around the lakes and rivers, but some were distanced from water bodies, such as the Lagazzi del Vho settlement found to the north of the Po Valley. The settlements to the south of the Po Valley offer little archaeological evidence, but it is evident they were densely settled during the Bronze Age. Scholars learn a lot from the mortuary rights of the peoples who inhabit a given area, but northern Italy lacks any burial evidence from the Bronze Age. Occasional human skulls or bones are discovered, but that is not enough to claim a spot as a necropolis. This suggests that the Polada culture had alternative ways of disposing of their dead, probably by exposure.

Other interesting aspects of the Polada culture are the sites that contain only one type of metalwork. These "hoards" are usually found outside of the settlement but nearby. They indicate extensive metalworking, and it is possible that the settlement traded with a specific type of item. The Savignano hoard consists of ninety-six flanged axes, which would suggest that the settlement produced them for trade with other peoples. These hoards are usually referred to as the "traders' hoards," as the items that have been found are both finished and unfinished. They were often made out of the same mold, and some of the stone molds were even found with the items. The settlements have produced finds of prestige items, such as amber or faience, but there is no evidence of social rankings among its population. This doesn't mean their society was equal, but rather that there is much more to discover.

However, evidence of social stratification can be found in central Italy. The eastern shores are characteristic of the Ripatransone culture, while the western shore was predominated by the Rinaldone culture. Both of these central Italian cultures show some evidence of social classification. Here, the tombs show different treatment of the bodies for different social statuses. Tomba della Vedova ("Tomb of the Widow") is a warrior chieftain burial site. He was buried together with his bride (she was probably sacrificed during the burial) and a dog who guards the entrance. For lesser warriors, weapons were sufficient enough to mark their social status in the afterlife.

Central Italy was predominantly pastoral land, so the economy of this region heavily relied on breeding and trading animals. Both the coastal plains and the uplands contained settlements known as "grazing camps," where people would bring their herds to graze in these grass-rich areas. These camps were simple, as they were not meant to be permanent settlements but rather seasonal stops. The permanent settlements of central Italy are either defended sites, such as Crostoletto di Lamone, with walls surrounding them, or cave-dwelling, valley bottom, or wetland sites.

The south of Italy was predominantly occupied by the Palma Campania culture. Here, the first cultivation of wine and olives started, but bronze artifacts are rare and occur mostly in burial sites. Social distinctions were very prominent. This can be seen in the items in the tombs. The few rich tombs that have been found, which contain bronze daggers and axes, differ from those containing common stone and clay items. Sicily was one of the first areas to start the progressive cultivation of fruit, which means that agriculture in this part of Italy was already at a higher level. Fruit cultivation requires high levels of labor input, something that would occur much later in the rest of Italy. The situation in the Lipari Islands (also known as the Aeolian Islands) was also unique. These islands, which are located between Sicily and mainland Italy, are filled with defensive settlements, which indicate some sort of conflict. The culture of these islands is very similar to that of the early Bronze Age Malta, and the conflict probably brought the new settlers to Italy.

Middle Bronze Age (c. 1700-1350 BCE)

The Middle Bronze Age began with the abandonment of the old settlements in the central Po Valley and the foundation of new ones immediately to the north. The number of settlements also increased drastically during this time, and they started showing the aspects of the Terramare culture. The name Terramare comes from the Italian *terra marna*, "the marl earth." Marl is a mudstone typically formed under freshwater conditions. It was on the mounds of this type of earth that the Terramare culture settlements were erected, hence the name. In the eastern part of the Po Valley, hilltop settlements can be found. These are known as *castellieri*, and they were typical for the regions east of Italy, such as Istria (today's Croatia). The *castellieri* were fortified settlements with a habitation area completely within the walls.

The northern areas of Italy began to see its first cremation burials during this period, but no social status is yet evident from the findings. There is a theory that the terramare houses built on poles (or piles) belonged to socially prominent individuals, but there is no evidence to support this claim. In the Venetian Plain, sword burials started, but it is believed they belonged to warriors, which wouldn't be a separate social rank on its own. These burial sites are also theorized to be connected with the culture emerging in the Danube-Carpathian region, as the burial styles are similar, and the tombs of both regions contain similar horse carvings made on deer antlers.

The Apennine culture was prominent in central and southern Italy during the Middle Bronze Age. Pastoral life developed further under their watch. Their settlements were established in a specific pattern, which was based on the need for the people to exploit both the lowlands and the highlands to survive. The lowlands contained the winter settlements, where the people would bring their cattle to graze during the snowy season. The highlands were perfect for their summer settlements, and the cattle were brought there to graze on the rich, grassy fields of the mountains. However, with the discovery of Luni sul Mignone in 1967, it is evident that this region also had sedentary settlements, where people preoccupied themselves with agriculture. It seems that the peoples of central and southern Italy were divided into two groups: the pastoral people, who would move their settlements seasonally, and the agricultural people, who had permanent settlements in the fertile lowlands. The existence of these two different types of people suggests economic diversity, which would have resulted in wealth for the region as a whole.

This transhumant pastoralism certainly played an important role in moving the Apennine culture through central and southern Italy. The fact that Apennine pottery, which was distinguished by its unique design, was found across a large geographical area shows that when people moved, so did the culture. The seasonal movement of people must have established social relations between different groups, which resulted in close cultural connections. There is little evidence for the social structure of the Middle Bronze Age in the central region, but two longhouses and three monumental tombs were found, showing the possible emergence of the elite class. Tomb 3 of Toppo Daguzzo contains up to ten human skeletons on its upper level. These people were buried without any ornaments or items. However, the lower level of the tomb contains eleven separate burials, of which six belong to males buried with weapons. Four belong to females, and some of them were buried with ornamental beads. The last burial place belongs to a child who was approximately five years old. The tomb was filled with other items, such as amber beads, pottery, and rock crystals. However, these items were scattered and couldn't be connected with any of the buried individuals.

Sicily and the islands between Sicily and Italy developed somewhat different settlements during the Middle Bronze Age. They started building circular and sub-circular buildings with roofs supported by a central pole. Later, the same settlements started constructing rectangular buildings, and many scholars believe that this was the period when the Sicilian settlements started showing the first signs of urbanization. The paved courtyards and streets, the stone walls, and the overall planning of settlements seem to indicate that some form of political structure existed. The most famous site with an early indication of urbanism is Thapsos, and it is believed that this settlement was a maritime trade center. The Thapsos culture had close contact with the Apennine culture of the mainland. This is demonstrated by the cultural influences they shared, which can be seen in pottery and other everyday items. But the early signs of trade that Thapsos had were unique, as several bronze vessels were found in its vicinity. These vessels, as well as some weapons found in the necropolis, are of Mycenaean culture (c. 1600–1100 BCE), the Greek culture of the Middle Bronze Age.

Recent Bronze Age (c. 1350–1150 BCE)

In both history and archaeology, the Bronze Age is divided into three main groups: Early, Middle, and Late. This classification is valid for all the English-speaking countries and their concept of history. However, when it comes to Italy, the changes it went through, as well as the emergence of different cultures, have led to different divisions of the Bronze Age. So, when it comes to Italian history, the Late Bronze Age is divided into two groups: Recent and Final.

The Recent Bronze Age of northern Italy saw the continuation of the Middle Bronze Age cultures but with the exponential growth of the settlements. During the previous period, the majority of settlements would surpass two hectares (between 200 to 400 individuals); in the Recent Bronze Age, the typical size was around five hectares (between 600 to 1,000 individuals). The preference for where to erect the new settlements also changed, as it seems the people now preferred dry land to the wetlands. However, a certain river cult continued to be practiced, although not much is known about it. It seems that this cult wasn't present in the central areas of northern Italy, which was predominantly wetlands. In the Po Valley, some terramare settlements were abandoned, but others grew beyond the average five hectares. For example, Fondo Paviani seems to have been around 16 hectares, while Case del Lago grew to an unbelievable 22.5 hectares. Some of these settlements even had inner fortified keeps that might have been the residence of the elite social class. However, some archaeologists argue that these fortified buildings are nothing more than community refuges for dangerous wartimes.

During the 1200s BCE, the central Po Valley was rapidly depopulated. There is no explanation for this occurrence, but some evidence suggests a catastrophic event (maybe an earthquake). Another explanation might be what is known in history as the Final Bronze Age collapse, which was when the cultures of the Eastern Mediterranean perished. But there is no evidence that the settlements of the Po Valley had any contact with the Eastern Mediterranean world at the time; however, they used a similar measurement system, so it is possible. The cause of this collective collapse of the most prominent empires in the Near East (the Mycenaean kingdoms, the Hittite Empire, Anatolia, the New Kingdom of Egypt, Levant, and many more) is unknown. It could be several factors: invasions, climate change, the eruption of volcanos, earthquakes, and so on. The consensus is that many factors influenced the Final Bronze Age collapse, and it is probably the same for the terramare settlements of northern Italy.

Central Italy went through a similar change during the Recent Bronze Age. The old sites were often abandoned, and people chose to relocate to naturally defendable locations, such as between hills or at the foot of the mountains. If the settlement survived, it increased its fortifications, which could be a sign of the elite class. There is evidence of huts that were larger than average, which probably belonged to individuals of higher social status. Some settlements expanded dramatically in Latium and Tuscany, and these areas started seeing a clear hierarchy. Some locations were simply more important, as they were near copper sources, while others were completely abandoned. Here, too, the river cult occurred, perhaps because metal deposits were heavily concentrated around rivers and lakes.

In southern Italy, the coastal villages transformed into ports. Many more sites took over the role of trading centers, such as Porto Perone and Scoglio del Tonno. Their primary clients were the Eastern Mediterranean kingdoms and empires. These settlements also show evidence of craft specialization. Each location produced a certain type of everyday item, which was later distributed further through trade. The locations in the mainland started showing increased defenses. New sites were almost always chosen because of their natural defensive abilities. But it seems that these inland settlements didn't enjoy the maritime trade or the development of the coastal ports. The olive cultivation intensified, and the storage jars were produced in the Aegean style. This suggests the existence of a redistributive economy or at least centralized storage, from which the whole community benefited.

The Final Bronze Age (c. 1150–950 BCE)

Italy went through drastic changes during the Final Bronze Age. The Proto-Villanovan culture appeared all over peninsular Italy, even down in the south, although it remained most concentrated in the north and the Po Valley. This specific culture strongly resembled the central European urn culture of the same period, and it is believed that it spread to the peninsula with the arrival of the proto-Italians. During the early period of the Final Bronze Age, some terramare settlements survived, especially in the northern Po Valley, but most of them were abandoned. The settlements that survived were no larger than sixteen hectares, and the everyday items found and dated to the Final Bronze Age indicates that there was contact with the Eastern Mediterranean. This is especially seen in the remains of Late Helladic pottery, which has been found in some of the sites. Archaeologists managed to confirm this theory by chemically analyzing the potsherds. But the results of the same chemical analysis done on bronze, bone, glass, and antler carvings showed that these items were of domestic production.

Frattesina is a Final Bronze Age settlement that was occupied continuously from the 12th century BCE until the 9th century BCE. It offers a unique view of the craftwork that was done on-site. Pottery, glass, ivory, bronze, and iron, as well as amber, bone, and antlers, all were worked and crafted there, and it seems that these items were traded with the Mediterranean world. Some of the raw materials, like amber and ivory, were imported, and the finished products were then exported. The necropolis of Frattesina offers little support for a social ranking system, but there are individuals buried with swords that may represent the settlement's elite.

Copper was supplied to Frattesina from the southern Alps and the central Italian region known as Tuscany today. These regions saw an increase in copper production, which is evident from the numerous findings of smelting sites. The use of these sites would continue in the Iron Age, showing continuity in the settlements of these regions. From Frattesina, the copper of the southern Alps and Tuscany found its way all over the Mediterranean world, mostly southern Italy, although it has also been found in the Near East and the central Mediterranean.

In central Italy, we start seeing the early formation of the states. However, those weren't the states as we know them today. The final transformation of the sites would occur in the Iron Age, but the Final Bronze Age testifies to settlement expansion and proto-cities. This is the time when the settlements in the lowlands started being abandoned, as the people started preferring higher grounds and natural defenses. This indicates the possibility of rivalry between groups and the existence of conflicts. The Proto-Villanovan settlements in central Italy were smaller than the ones in the north. They mostly occupied hilltops and rarely exceeded five hectares. The cemeteries accompanying the settlements are also small and offer no evidence of social ranks. However, some of the villages, such as Nuccia Negroni Catacchio, have separate areas of the hilltop where an elite class might have lived. The necropolis of Pianello di Genga is an exception to the norm, as it is quite big. It contains over 500 graves, but this site was in use over the centuries, so it probably served more than just one group of people.

Southern Italy also started changing. Graves became decorated with more metalwork than in previous times. These were mostly weapons, which might mean the settlements saw an increased need for warriors, or it might mean there was an emergence of an elite warrior class. In Sicily, we see early iron-working during the Final Bronze Age. The site where an iron spearhead was found belonged to a group of people who defended their settlement with a stone wall and a ditch. A similar iron spearhead was found in today's Albania, where a large graveyard of warriors was found. However, Sicily also offered a finding of two knives made from iron at the Madonna del Piano cemetery in Molino della Badia.

Chapter 2 – Iron Age and Pre-Roman Italy

At the end of the Final Bronze Age and the beginning of the Iron Age (c. 900–700 BCE), Italy had a population with many different origins. There was a sudden increase of migrations into the peninsula, but information about it is still obscured, so we can only guess where these peoples came from. Nevertheless, the influx of new peoples is evident, and scholars speculate about the two main routes of migration into Italy. One was the sea route, which leads from the Balkans across the Adriatic Sea, and the other was the land route via the northern Balkans and central Europe. The Iapygians (Apulians) came through the first route. The Iapygians were an Indo-European group of people who settled in southeastern Italy (today's Apulia). The Indo-Europeans of the Pontic steppe (on the northern coast of the Black Sea) came via the second route. They entered Italy through the northeast and then spread into groups that settled on either side of the Italian coastline. These Indo-Europeans became the Italic peoples.

By 800 BCE, Italy was settled by three main groups of peoples: the Iapygians, the Italics, and the Etruscans. As far as speculations go, the Iapygians were the Illyrian tribes that crossed the Adriatic Sea from today's Dalmatia in the 12th or 11th century BCE. The Italics came a century later, although some scholars believe that it was the other way around and that the Italics were already settled on the peninsula when the Iapygians arrived. This could suggest that the Italics didn't come in only one migration wave. In fact, it is believed that there were two main migrations of the Italic peoples, and with them came their relatives, the Latins. It is believed that several hundreds of years separate the two main migration waves, but that doesn't mean there weren't any movements of peoples between them. The Italics are believed to have origins in the northern Balkans, and they arrived on the Apennine Peninsula through today's Slovenia.

The Iapygians in southern Italy fragmented into several tribes and continued to move toward the eastern shores. The Italics broke into two main groups: the Opici (Osci) and Umbri. As time passed, these two groups continued to fragment further. The Umbri became the main inhabitants of central Italy; even today, the area is known as Umbria. In the central regions of Italy, the Illyrians arrived and pushed the Italic tribes toward the south of the peninsula. At the same time, around the 8th century BCE, Greeks started colonizing the Italian shores, and they pushed the settled peoples inland, as well as farther to the west and south. The Itali and Siculi tribes were finally pushed into Calabria, and they started inhabiting the island of Sicily. These migrations, fragmentations of groups, and the Greek colonization are the beginnings of Italian history. Soon, Rome would rise, along with the first historians, who traveled the peninsula and recorded the peoples and tribes they found. Eventually, they would all be Latinized and conquered by the ever-expanding Romans.

The Etruscans

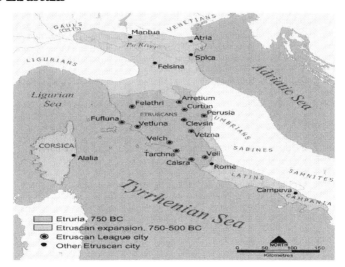

The Etruscan civilization and their neighbors

https://en.wikipedia.org/wiki/Etruscan_civilization#/media/
File:Etruscan_civilization_map.png

The Etruscans were a group of people who came to the Apennine Peninsula, and they were the only ones without Indo-European ancestry. They were completely different from the rest of the tribes inhabiting Italy at the time, but they were powerful and influential. Modern linguists and historians believe that it was the Etruscans who shaped Rome and allowed it to become one of the most powerful empires in the world. They influenced Roman culture, language, and belief systems. The Etruscan language is now dead and forgotten, but through their influence on Latin, we are still using some old Etruscan words, for example, people, arena, military, and even Rome. Today, it is believed that Rome wasn't named by its mythological founders Romulus and Remus but, in fact, by the Etruscan tribe that founded it, the Ruma tribe.

The origin of the Etruscans remains unknown. There are many theories, and they are as old as the ancient Greek historian Herodotus, who described the arrival of the Etruscans. But Herodotus wasn't a contemporary, as he wrote about these mysterious people in the 5th century BCE. According to him, the Etruscans came to Italy around 800 BCE when a famine in Lydia (today's Turkey) broke out. The king of Lydia divided his people into two groups and ordered them to draw lots to determine which group would stay and which one would leave the country in search of a better life. The castaway group traveled the world and eventually arrived in Italy. Unfortunately, Herodotus is known for believing myths and legends to be founded in historical truth. The contemporaries of this ancient historian named him "the storyteller." He was even given the title "father of lies," as his history theories are not always to be trusted.

But it was linguists who discovered the similarities between the old Etruscan language and some of the old languages of today's regions in Turkey. Scholars all over the world are researching the Etruscans and their connections to ancient Lydia. But the connections between the Etruscans and Lydians are not only linguistic. Some of their customs are too similar to ignore. For example, both peoples practiced Herosposy, the study of a sacrificed animal's entrails to foresee the will of the gods. However, it seems that the Etruscans and Lydians didn't believe in the same gods, which is another thing that puzzles modern scholars. Most of the archaeological evidence shows no connection between the two peoples, and it seems that archaeology prefers the theory that the Etruscans were indigenous to Italy. The material culture and the social practices of the two peoples are completely different, and it is possible that Herodotus and other ancient historians who assumed there was a connection between the Etruscans and ancient Lydians based it solely on the evidence that there was some kind of trade and cultural exchange between the Greeks and Etruscans.

Some DNA tests were performed on the remains of the ancient Etruscans, but the results were either inconclusive or no specific haplogroups were found that connect the Etruscans with any other group of people in Europe. Some evidence emerged in 2007 that the people who live in the Etruscan areas today have some genetic similarity with the Turkish people, but this is explained by the modern connection between the Italians and Turks. The DNA evidence, just as the archaeological evidence, seems to favor the theory that the Etruscans were indigenous to Italy. Their civilization occurred around 800 BCE, but it seems that the people who started it were much older. The cultural evidence is very strong, and it tells a story of the existence of a continuous culture in the regions of Etruria from the Final Bronze Age until deep into the Iron Age. The Proto-Villanovan culture morphed into the Villanova culture of the Etruscans, so it seems that the Etruscan ancestors occupied Italy before the emergence of their civilization in the 800s.

The Villanovan Culture

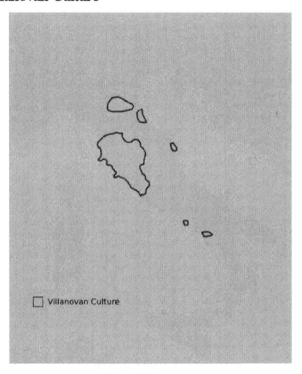

The Villanovans

The Villanovan culture of the Iron Age directly followed the Bronze Age Proto-Villanovan culture of central Italy. The Villanovans are now regarded as possible ancestors of the Etruscans, as there is no historical or archaeological evidence that the two peoples clashed in warfare or that an alien group of people migrated into the territory of the Villanovans. There is nothing to suggest that the Villanovans were different from the Etruscans. The culture itself saw sudden prosperity when the people started exploiting the natural goods more extensively. Villages formed, and people constructed rectangular and circular houses out of wooden strips and daub and fashioned straw roofs on top. There were wooden and terracotta decorations added to the structures. Many terracotta urns were found in the early Etruscan sites, which indicate that this civilization burned their dead from its beginnings.

The Villanovan culture is famous for its urns that resemble their houses. The urns were intentionally made in such a shape, as the soul of the deceased needed housing in the afterlife. The urns were even made with the added chimneys and some crude imitations of the real house's decorations. Typical geometric patterns on the walls of the urns and the roof imitate the typical Etruscan architecture of the later period. These urns closely resemble the ones found in the Iron Age archaeological sites of Germany and Romania, but there is no further evidence to suggest a deeper connection.

To the Villanovans, the most important animal was probably the horse. This can be observed through the archaeological findings of numerous horse fittings and from the frequent occurrence of this animal in their art. The bronze work of the early Villanovans is of very high quality, which suggests a dedication to this metalworking art. The population increased over time, and the villages turned into towns. Cemeteries had to be expanded. During this time, it is believed the Villanovans had a societal elite. New items were added to the graves, such as miniature chairs, housewares, armor, and weapons for men and weaving equipment for women. All of these items confirm that the Villanovans believed in some kind of afterlife, but a strange thing happened. Archaeologists found that some female graves contained armor and weapons and that some male graves had weaving paraphernalia. It seems that gender roles were not set in stone for the Villanovans; it is believed the women had a more active role in society, while men were included in clothes production.

With the boom in population and the expansion of towns came the first conflicts, as the competition for the natural resources was severe. Some tribes decided to move away from the center and occupy areas in the north and south of central Italy. Some evidence suggests that during the Early Iron Age, some Villanovans settled in western Italy too. The first evidence of trade emerged, and it started between different Villanovan towns and villages. It quickly spread to the wider Mediterranean world, as the Greeks started founding their colonies alongside the Italian coast in the mid-8th century BCE. Greek pottery and metalwork started occurring in Villanovan sites, confirming the trade theory. Soon the locals started imitating not only Greek production but also their culture and belief system as well.

Through trade connections with Greece, the Villanovan culture made contact with the Near East and Phoenicia. These peoples made a deep impression on the Villanovan culture, which started maturing into the Etruscan culture. This first happened in the south, near the Greek colonies, but it spread northward very quickly. The Villanovan culture sprouted out of the Proto-Villanovan culture, but it could also be easily named the Proto-Etruscan culture, as it continued to evolve until the 7th and early 6th centuries BCE. The Etruscans continued to prosper up until the 2nd century BCE when they were assimilated by the Romans.

Etruria

The cities of the Etruscan people were independent. They were not connected by a common administration or rule. Each of them was a different city-state, and the only thing they had in common was their culture, religion, and language. The territory that contained the

Etruscan cities spread from the Tiber River in the south to the Po Valley in the north (together with some parts of the Po Valley). Some of the major Etruscan cities were Veii, Populonia, and Cerveteri. Because of the great independence of these cities, developments in architecture, art, and manufacturing emerged at different times in different places. The coastal cities had greater contact with the rest of the Mediterranean world and developed at a much faster rate than the cities situated inland. Eventually, the coastal cities would pass on the contemporary culture to others through trade.

Central Italy was fertile, so agriculture flourished. It was also rich in iron mines, which were exploited by the Etruscans, who developed high-quality tools. But they also improved the production of pottery and other products, as they could be traded across the sea. They extensively traded in gold and silver with the Greeks, Carthaginians, and Phoenicians. They developed an extensive trade network across the Mediterranean, as well as between other Etruscan cities. This network extended to the tribes of northern Italy and farther into central Europe.

The evidence suggests Etruscans imported slaves, manufactured goods, and raw materials, and they exported iron, pottery, wine, olive oil, pine nuts, and grain. Trade flourished from the 7th BCE onward, and that is when the cultural impact of the Greek settlers was the strongest. The Etruscans easily picked up Greek clothing, eating habits, religion, and the Greek alphabet. This is what is known as the Orientalizing period in Etruscan history.

But with increased trade came competition and their first conflicts. There is evidence of an alliance between the Etruscans and Carthaginians against the Greek naval force, which took place somewhere around 540 BCE. The Battle of Alalia took place near Corsica, and the Greeks defeated the alliance easily. However, the Etruscans were still a major trading competitor, and Greeks often referred to them as the "Scoundrel Pirates." Another battle occurred in 474, this time between the Etruscans and Syracusans, who had become the dominant force behind trade in the Mediterranean world. At the Battle of Cumae, the Etruscans suffered another defeat, but they hadn't seen the worst of the Syracusans yet. In 384 BCE, the tyrant Dionysius I of Syracuse decided to directly attack the Etruscan coast and destroy their ports. These defeats contributed to the gradual decline of the Etruscans' trading power and their culture as well.

In the Etruscan hinterland, warfare was different. The evidence suggests that the inland Etruscan cities followed the Greek example of a soldier. They wore bronze breastplates, headgear similar to the Corinthians, and greaves, and they wielded a large circular shield. Several chariots have been discovered in the Etruscan tombs, but it is not known if these were used in warfare or if they had a strictly ceremonial use. There is evidence that Etruscans used mercenaries to fight for them, but there is nothing conclusive. The cities improved their defenses by erecting tall walls, towers, and strong gates. This evolution of the cities indicates that the Etruscans faced a new threat from the south, which was where the Latins would soon build a great empire. The Romans were on their way to conquer Etruria.

While Rome was just a lesser neighbor of the Etruscans in the 6th century, it started developing quickly, and by the 4th century BCE, it was showing off its power. At the time, legends rose of the Etruscan kings ruling over Rome, but there is no evidence to confirm these myths. The Etruscans continued to weaken, and not only because of the Syracusan attacks on their harbors. The Celtic tribes from the north started invading central Italy during the 5th, 4th, and 3rd centuries BCE. Sometimes, the Celts would even ally with the Etruscans against Rome, but most of the time, they would invade, pillaging and looting the lands before quickly retreating. For over 200 years, central Italy suffered constant attacks by various enemies. The Etruscan cities were conquered by Rome, which would be followed by peace treaties and temporary alliances. Then the warfare would begin again, and the sieges of the cities would continue. One lasted for ten years; Rome besieged Veii in 406 BCE, and the siege only ended in 396 with the final Battle of Veii. Rome broke the siege by digging tunnels underneath the city walls. Veii finally fell, and its citizens were massacred or enslaved. Eventually, the city was repopulated by the Romans.

Rome had a superior army, one with greater tactical skills and manpower. Two more battles occurred between the Romans and the Etruscans when the cities of Chiusi and Sentinum fell in 295 BCE. The problem with the Etruscan cities was that they had no political unity, and they also never agreed to ally with each other and organize a defense against Rome. In 280 BCE, Tarquinia fell, which had been the greatest trading city of the Etruscans since the 8th century BCE. After its fall, the Romans had no problems taking Orvieto, Vulci, and other Etruscan cities. Cerveteri was one of the last cities to fall, doing so in 273 BCE, and with it, the Etruscan civilization came to an end. But was it the end of the whole culture?

At the time, the Romans had a habit of slaughtering enemy civilians and inhabiting the newly conquered places with their own people. This ensured the well-being of the ever-growing Roman population. The professional army of Rome was organized in such a way that the veterans were promised land from the conquered territories. To reward its soldiers, Rome had to expel the old population. The veterans and their families would work these lands and produce foodstuffs for Rome.

Even though Rome didn't allow itself to be conquered militarily, it was conquered culturally. The Romans absorbed the cultures of the peoples they warred with, and the Etruscans probably had the biggest influence on them. From their Etruscan neighbors, the Romans took over not only their artistic style but also their belief system. Through the Etruscans, Rome was influenced by the Greek colonies of Italy. But the Latin language was never replaced by Etruscan. Latin became the main language of the whole peninsula. However, the Latins did borrow a few words from the Etruscans, and some of them, as we saw, are in use even today. Although Etruscan literature and history were obliterated after the conquest, the culture continued to live, even though it was changed to fit the Roman narrative. By 80 BCE, there were no more Etruscans, but their religious practices, art, fashionable togas, temples, armor, augurs, and victory processions continued to live through the Romans. This is why scholars believe the Etruscans never really disappeared. They may have been assimilated, but they were able to influence their conquerors.

Chapter 3 – Italy in the Roman Period

Rome first appeared in the 8th century BCE. Its citizens believed that the city was founded by two brothers, Romulus and Remus, who were raised by a she-wolf. The ancient Romans even celebrated April 21st as the day when their city was first founded, but this date cannot be confirmed. The legend tells the story of how Romulus killed his brother Remus over an argument about where the city should be located. This legend of Rome's beginning is well known around the world, and Romulus and Remus still have statues commemorating them as the fathers of the modern civilized world. However, many stories surround the foundation of the city, and this is just a small part of it. The Romans believed they were the descendants of King Aeneas, who survived the fall of Troy. He was the ancestor of the twin brothers Romulus and Remus, so, indirectly it was Aeneas who was the father of all Romans. But other theories about the foundation of the city have emerged in modern history.

Rome might be of Etruscan origin, as it has been suggested that the city was named after the Etruscan tribe Ruma, who possibly migrated southward. Even legends of ancient Rome mention Etruscan kings ruling the city in its early days. It is also possible that the city was named Rome due to the ancient Etruscan name for the Tiber River, *Rumon*. However, Rome has been continuously inhabited since the 8th century BCE. With old cities such as this one, it is hard to separate fact from legend. It is possible we will never fully learn its true origins and who was its founder.

At first, Rome was ruled by kings. The legends name seven ancient kings of Rome, from Romulus to Tarquin. During their rule, the city grew, mainly due to trade. The location of Rome was perfect, as the waterway of the Tiber River opened the way for merchants to access the rest of the Mediterranean. The Romans were heavily influenced by the Greek colonies to the south, from which they based their religion, literacy, and architecture, but it was the influence of the Etruscan civilization that refined this culture and turned it into what would be the Roman civilization. Between the 8th and 6th centuries BCE, Rome grew exponentially, and its citizens continued to trade, but they also turned to production. The Romans were masters of borrowing other people's skills and inventions and further developing them.

At the end of the 6th century, the Romans were dissatisfied with the way their kings ruled. There are many myths that explain the fall of the monarchy and the rise of the republic. When King Tarquin the Proud was deposed, his successor, Lucius Junius Brutus, reformed the government and established the Roman Republic. He was also the first consul of Rome and the ancestor of Marcus Junius Brutus, who killed the most famous Roman figure, Gaius Julius Caesar. Modern scholars disagree with the mythological story of the end of the Roman monarchy. They believe the Etruscan invasion deposed King Tarquin. However, the citizens successfully defended the city from this invasion.

In 509, the year when the monarchy was supposedly overthrown, the Romans declared they would never allow one man to rule the city. Instead, they came up with the consulship, which was shared between two people. These men could hold power for only one year, after which two new consuls would be chosen. But it wasn't the people who chose the consuls. In fact, the Roman Republic was never really a democracy. It was ruled by powerful families, whose members were senators, and they were a driving force behind the politics of the city. The senators chose who would occupy the high positions, and they had the power to oversee their rule. Over time, senators gained and lost some of their power, but the citizens continued to be divided by class. The ruling class was called the Optimates, which can be loosely translated as "the best men," while the lower classes were simply called the Populares, "favoring the people." The two classes weren't only social divisions; they were also a political one. Some members of the Optimates would support the cause of the people, and they were given the designation Populares too. Generally speaking, the political differences between the two parties were very simple. The Optimates supported the idea of social classification and the idea that the Senate should hold the ultimate power, while the Populares believed in democracy and the equality of all Roman citizens.

Once the new governmental system was in place, Rome showed its tendency to expand through warfare.

Rome's Neighbors

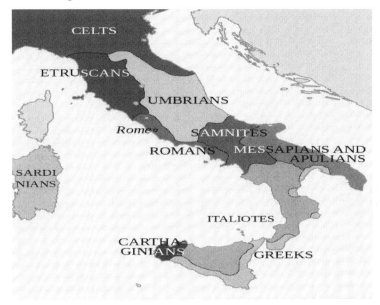

Today's Italy in 400 BCE

https://en.wikipedia.org/wiki/Ancient_Rome#/media/File:Italy_400bC_en.svg

The Latins

The earliest citizens of Rome were the Latins. Latium is the ancient area around the Alban Hills; it extends toward the south, all the way to Mount Circeo. This whole area of Latium was inhabited by the Italic tribe of Latins, and Rome was just one of their settlements. During the early days of the Roman conquest, these Latins were the city's immediate neighbors, and they were the first to be conquered in a series of conflicts known as the Roman-Latin wars. Like the Etruscans, various Latin cities were connected only by their culture and religion. They probably traded with each other, as well as outside of their region. However, there was no political unity between them until Rome became powerful enough to assert its dominance over all of Latium.

The old Latium, which was how this region was referred to by the Romans, had Etruria as its northern neighbor and Umbria to the south. Their western border was the Tyrrhenian Sea. Just as with the Romans, the Latins were greatly influenced by the Etruscans. From them, they learned how to read and write and how to organize and standardize the military. The first ruler of the Latins was King Latinus. Latinus is a mythological figure, and he was also a participant in the Trojan War. Latinus is known to the Greeks from their legends about Troy, but it was the Romans who continued his story and made him the forefather of all Latins. In the mythological episode of the foundation of Rome and the kidnapping of the Sabine women, the Latins fought against Romulus and his band, allying themselves with the Sabines. This early conflict probably occurred in 753 BCE, the same year that Rome was founded.

The settlements of the Latins were various, and each settlement was considered a different tribe (or clan). The first Latin tribe, which was conquered by the Dardanian refugees of the Trojan War, was the Rutuli. The Crustumni people founded the settlement of Crustumerium, and they were the ones who allied with the Sabines against Rome. The Camineri inhabited the Alban Hills, and they were conquered by the alliance of the Romans and Sabines sometime between 753 and 748 BCE. There were also the Latins who lived in Alba Longa, but there is not much known about them. It seems they were quiet, non-military people who were simply absorbed into Rome. Early sources mention around thirty Latin settlements, but by the 500s, that number was reduced to only fifteen independent cities. Rome was included as one of the cities of Old Latium, but soon enough, it became the only city, as the others were annexed after its expansion.

It seems that not all Latins equally accepted the dominance of Rome. Some cities, even though they were annexed early during the Roman Republic, often rebelled and tried to regain their independence. In 503, according to the Roman historian Livy, the towns of Pometia and Cora allied themselves with the Aurunci, a southern Latin tribe. Together, they tried to revolt against Rome, but they ultimately failed. These kinds of attempts occurred until the 4th century, which was when the Latin War took place. This conflict lasted from 340 to 338, during which Latins united with the Volsci people and tried to break off from Rome. The Latins were unsuccessful. When the peace treaty was signed, Rome managed to annex some of the Latin territories, while the others finally gained their autonomy.

The Sabines

The Sabines were a mountain-dwelling Italic tribe. They occupied the slopes of the Apennine Mountains before the foundation of Rome. However, it seems that the Sabine population was divided at one point, and while the larger portion of the tribe remained in the mountains, some of them moved to the south and inhabited the area of Latium, just above Rome. The stories surrounding the Sabines are closely related to the myth about the founding of Rome. It is said that when Romulus founded the city, he invited rebels, exiles, and criminals to occupy Rome as its first citizens. They came, but they were alone. They had no families and no wives. Because they lacked women, Romulus ordered his people to attack the Sabines and kidnap their daughters. This legend of the Sabine women is engraved in cultures around the world, as the scene is still reproduced in various art forms today, from paintings to literature. But the Sabine men wouldn't simply give up on their women. A war followed, during which many lives were lost. The women, who were now married to Roman men, wouldn't stand for this kind of killing, as it affected both their new husbands and their old husbands and family members. Their intervention brought the war to an end. The Sabine women agreed to become Roman women, and a new alliance between the Romans and the Sabines was organized.

It is believed that the myth about the kidnapping of the Sabine women was nothing more than political propaganda of the later period. Rome was supposedly ruled by two kings after the war ended: Romulus and King Titus Tatius of the Sabines. Historically, the Sabines merged with the Romans, and they founded one nation. Many Romans were proud of their Sabine ancestry, and many of them became emperors of Rome later. But today, all we know about the Sabines is that they were an Indo-European people who came to Italy, perhaps even before the Latins. Their origins remain unknown, although early historians speculate they were sent from the ancient Kingdom of Lacedaemon (later renamed Sparta) to found a colony in Italy. Because of this, the Sabines are thought to have Spartan origins, but it is possible that the ancient historians simply connected the Sabines' love for warfare, aggressiveness, and bluntness with the Spartan culture.

No inscriptions of strictly Sabine origin have ever been found. It is believed they spoke the Oscan language, as the Latin writers noted some of their words as being of Sabine origin. The legend of the Sabine women is mythological in origin, but it has a historical value, as Rome often warred with the Sabines during the 4th and 3rd centuries BCE. The alliance between the two peoples is also probably accurate, but it doesn't necessarily mean that the rule was shared. Modern history believes that Rome was victorious in the conflict with the Sabines in 449. After that, the Sabines don't show up in any Roman records until 290, when they were conquered and assimilated into Roman culture. The Sabines received full Roman citizenship by 268, and that was when they stopped existing as a nation. Their Latinization and absorption into the Roman world were completed by the 1st century CE. Only the memory of the Sabines continues to survive.

The Samnites

The southern neighbors of Rome were the Samnites, another Oscan-speaking group of people. It is believed the Samnites were a group of Sabines who continued the migration from the Apennine Mountains by moving farther south, inhabiting the region known as Safinium. In Latin, this region is called Samnium, which was how the name Samnites came about. The modern province of Benevento is only a portion of what Samnium used to be, but the ancient borders fluctuated so often that it is impossible to talk about any permanent borders.

The region of Samnium was inhabited by four tribes: the Pentri, Carricini, Caudini, and Irpini. These tribes formed a confederation and were collectively known as the Samnites. It is possible that at later dates, other tribes joined the confederation. The Pentri were settled in the very heart of Samnium. They were tough, war-loving people, and they were the foundation of the Samnite confederation. The Carricini occupied the northern regions of Samnium, and their population was very sparse. The Caudini lived to the west and were influenced by the Greeks. The Irpini were the southerners among the Sabines, and they were often called *uomini lupo* by the Romans, which means the "wolf people." In fact, their Oscan name was *hirpus*, which means "wolf."

Most of the Samnites were sheepherders, and the culture itself knew no slavery. But they displayed a certain love for conflict, as they organized war-like games during their festivities. These games would later become a common practice throughout Rome, as it would bring about the rise of the gladiators. The first records of the Samnites in the written sources are about their victory over the Roman army in 321 BCE. They conquered some of the Roman territories, expanding their rule, and they reached the peak of their expansion in 316 BCE. However, a series of conflicts with Rome soon followed, in which the Samnites lost. Their power was broken by 290, and the Samnites started appearing in the ranks of the Roman army. But some of the Samnite people remained rebellious, and instead of surrendering to

Rome, they decided to join Hannibal Barca in his efforts during the Second Punic War (218-201 BCE). Those who stayed loyal to Rome were integrated into society but were refused citizenship. To advance in social and political life, one needed official citizenship, and the Samnites soon rebelled, starting the Social War (91-87 BCE). During this period, Lucius Cornelius Sulla became the dictator, and even though he was the enemy of the rebels, he granted the Samnites Roman citizenship to prevent further conflicts. The process of complete assimilation began, and there are no more mentions of the Samnites as a people in the Roman record. However, some of the more notable Romans were proud of their Samnite heritage, among them being the famous Cassius Longinus and Pontius Pilate, who ordered the crucifixion of Jesus.

The Gauls

The Gauls are a Celtic people, and they came to Italy during the 4th century, crossing the Alps from France. This is why the Gauls who settled in Italy are known as the Cisalpine Gauls and are differentiated from the Transalpine Gauls, who lived in some regions of France. But the Gauls were not a single people. They were merely a Celtic group of peoples, and there were many individual tribes within the overarching Gauls, such as Boii, Carni, Cenomani, Insubres, and Orobii. They crossed the Alps as early as the 13th century BCE, and they settled in the western regions of the Po Valley, where they merged with the indigenous peoples to form the Golasecca culture. Around the 6th century, these Gallic tribes were again on the move, and while crossing the Alps, located in the western part of Italy, they met with the Ligurians. The two peoples mixed, and the Ligurians soon became Celticized, which is evident from the changes in their language. However, this linguistic hypothesis is based on the names of old settlements that still thrive in some regions. The old Ligurian language was not preserved, and it is not known when exactly it took its Celtic form. The northeastern part of Italy was inhabited by the Veneti people. The movement of the Gauls into their territory brought the rapid loss of the Veneti culture, and by the 4th century, these indigenous people were completely assimilated into the Gallic culture. They kept their language, but other than that, they couldn't be discerned from the Gauls.

In the 4th century BCE, the second wave of the Gaul migration occurred, and once more, the Gallic tribes of France crossed the Alps and entered the northernmost region of Italy. But this time, they didn't stop in the far north; instead, they occupied the vast territory between the Alps and the Apennines. Here, the first contact with Rome occurred, and it was one of war and conflict. In 390, the first battle between the Romans and Gauls, specifically the Senones tribe, was fought. The Romans lost the Battle of the Allia, and the Senones even managed to sack Rome. The Romans paid off the Gauls to leave the city, but that wasn't the end of the conflict between the two peoples. The Gauls would prove to be a much more resourceful enemy and a constant nuance to the Romans, even during the Roman Empire.

Rome's Expansion into the Mediterranean

By the 3rd century BCE, Rome was the superior power in Italy. It had conquered and absorbed many of its neighbors, but it had not yet tested its military power against Carthage or Greece, the rulers of the Mediterranean world. Rome had no intention of fighting Greece; it even had a treaty with the Greek colonies in Italy (known as Magna Graecia). This treaty prohibited Roman vessels from entering the Tarentine Gulf, where one of the most important Greek colonies, Tarentum, overlooked the sea. Roman ships eventually entered the forbidden waters, although it was supposedly only as a military response to another Italic people, the Lucanians. But the Greeks didn't trust this excuse, and since they felt threatened, they chose to sink the Roman ships. Fearing the retaliation that would certainly come, the Greeks invited Pyrrhus, the king of Epirus, to fight the Romans in their stead. Pyrrhus saw the Greek invitation as an excuse to found his own colony in Italy, maybe even an empire. In 280 BCE, the first conflicts began with the Battle of Heraclea. Pyrrhus defeated the Romans because his army used elephants, which the Romans had not seen in battle before. But they quickly adapted, and even though they did not have sufficient power to defeat Pyrrhus in the Battle of Asculum (279 BCE), they managed to inflict such losses to his army that the term "Pyrrhic victory" was coined. This term is used to define a victory that costs more than it's worth.

Pyrrhus never finished his campaign against the Romans because the same year, the Greeks of Sicily invited him to take the rule and drive off the Carthaginians, who were attacking the island. Pyrrhus successfully fought the Carthaginians in Sicily until 276, but the inhabitants of the island were unsatisfied with his rule. They hated him so much that they were willing to invite the Carthaginians back. At this point, Pyrrhus contemplated running back to Epirus, but he received the news that Rome continued its conquest over the Greek colonies on the mainland. Only Tarentum still stood, and it was calling Pyrrhus for help. The king saw this call as yet another opportunity to establish his presence in Italy, and he departed the Sicilian shore. However, at the Strait of Messina, the Carthaginian armada attacked his ship. Pyrrhus reached Italy's mainland with only 12 ships remaining out of 110. He had no manpower to fight Rome, but he dared to answer the challenge on one occasion: the Battle of Beneventum (275 BCE). Reinforced by the Greeks and some of the Italic tribes, such as the Messapians and Lucanians, Pyrrhus fought bravely, and the outcome of the battle was indecisive. Realizing that Rome had grown to become a tremendous power, Pyrrhus decided to abandon his ambitions in Italy. He was also aware of the brewing conflict between Rome and Carthage, and it was probably a wise decision to leave and not be in the middle when the two giants decided to cross swords.

The Punic Wars

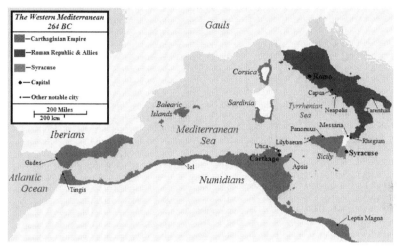

Rome and Carthage before the First Punic War

https://en.wikipedia.org/wiki/Punic_Wars#/media/
File:First_Punic_War_264_BC_v3.png

Carthage was one of the oldest and strongest Mediterranean powers of the ancient world. It emerged in the 9th century BCE as a Phoenician colony. It occupied the territory of today's Tunisia and southern Spain. This geographical position allowed Carthage to thrive and grow. By the 3rd century, it was so powerful that it could simply ban Romans from entering the waters of the western Mediterranean. Any Roman trade ship caught in these waters was destined to sink. At the time, Rome had no navy, and it only spread its influence through Italy. But Rome showed a tendency to conquer, and it was only a matter of time before the city would need access to the whole Mediterranean to satisfy its trade needs.

The territory that sparked the conflict between the two Mediterranean powers was Sicily. Once it was abandoned by King Pyrrhus, the island was shared by Rome and Carthage. But Syracuse was an independent Greek colony, and since 289 BCE, they had been suffering constant attacks by the Mamertines, an Italian group of mercenaries. But the Mamertines were unable to conquer the city alone. Soon, they asked both Carthage and Rome for help. Carthage accepted the call, but after hearing that their soon-to-be allies also invited Rome, they turned their backs to the Mamertines and sided with Hiero II of Syracuse. Rome agreed to help the mercenaries conquer the Greek city, and in 264 BCE, the first war between Carthage and Rome was declared.

Rome still had no navy, but it knew that in order to successfully fight Carthage, maritime warfare was the only answer. Three hundred thirty ships were quickly built, and the Roman generals, who were used to land battles, devised a new tactic for fighting on the water. Their ships were equipped with a clever device, a movable plank called a *corvus*, which could be attached to the enemy ship and serve as a bridge for soldiers to board and fight on the enemy's deck. The Romans were famous for quickly adapting, and this was one of their genius ways to implement already-known land battle tactics to maritime fights.

During the first conflicts, the Romans were not as successful as they had hoped. They still lacked the experience of fighting on the seas, and they had no general who could successfully command the armada. Carthage, on the other hand, knew very well how to fight on the waters, and they employed one of their best generals, Hamilcar Barca (275-228 BCE), to strike down the Roman coastal cities. This left the Romans already occupied in battle without a supply line. But the leaders of Carthage underestimated the Romans, as they thought Barca would be capable of fighting them alone. While he was successful during the first conflict and won a major victory at Drepana in 249 BCE, Barca soon found himself lacking manpower and supplies. Both armies were exhausted, and the fighting was paused for the next seven years. During that time, the leaders of Carthage accumulated wealth, still believing Rome wasn't a real threat. The Romans used those seven years to build 200 battleships and to recruit over 60,000 troops.

The war continued in 241 BCE, and the Romans won a series of decisive victories, surprising their enemy with their renewed strength.

Carthage still didn't want to send help to General Barca, who had to rely on employed mercenaries. The final battle, the Battle of the Aegates, was fought in March of 241, and the Romans, having the better-trained and better-equipped army, won. Barca asked Carthage yet again for help, but instead, the Carthaginian Senate sent orders to sue for peace with Rome. Carthage failed to preserve its dominance over the Mediterranean Sea, lost its part of Sicily, and had to pay reparations to Rome. But the leaders of the once-great civilization also failed to pay the mercenaries who fought for them, which would prove to be a big mistake.

The days of the old and powerful Carthage were over. While it could still boast its significance in the Mediterranean world, the civilization itself was overly indulged in corruption and internal power play. The funds that should have gone to the military were stolen by the Carthaginian senators, whose only interest was to fill their own pockets. When the time came for Carthage to pay the mercenaries who had fought on their side against Rome, the city treasury was almost empty. The Senate simply refused to pay, and the insulted mercenaries decided to attack the city. Once more, the Carthaginians relied on the military genius of Hamilcar Barca to free the city. But the Senate still refused to invest in the military, and what was supposed to be quick relief of Carthage ended up being the four-year-long Mercenary War (241-237 BCE). Rome took the opportunity to seize the Carthaginian colonies of Corsica and Syracuse, and the Carthaginians didn't even bother to retake them. Once the Mercenary War was over, they focused on conquering Spain, but Rome was already there, taking the territories north of the Ebro River and setting the scene for the Second Punic War (218-201 BCE).

Hamilcar Barca died in 228 BCE, and he was succeeded as the military leader of the Spanish conquest by his son-in-law, Hasdrubal the Fair. But Hasdrubal lived only a few years longer, dying in 221, and he was succeeded by Hannibal Barca, Hamilcar's son. Legend has it that when Hannibal was just a boy, his father made him swear an oath that he would fight Rome. In 219, Hannibal marched the Carthaginian army north of the Ebro River into the territory of Rome. He attacked the Iberian city of Saguntum, which was under the protection of Rome. This provoked Rome, and the senators declared war on Carthage in the spring of 219 BCE. But Hannibal was clever, and he was able to gather a huge army, accompanied by war elephants, which he took over the Alps and into Italy. Rome didn't expect that; they never believed the war would come to their doorstep. The proper invasion of Roman territories had begun. The Second Punic War is remembered in history as one of the bloodiest wars ever. Not only did many soldiers lose their lives, but whole cities were obliterated, and civilians were massacred or enslaved. During the seventeen-year-long war, the whole Mediterranean world was affected. No one was safe.

Hannibal was victorious in many of his initial battles, and his name inspired fear in the Roman citizens. They were afraid their city was next, and they believed that if Hannibal came, Rome would certainly fall. Rome quickly reinforced the city's walls and recruited additional forces for the defense of the city. Hannibal saw no reason to attack Rome directly. He knew Italy would fall if he took other cities. Ticinus, Trebia, and Trasimene fell, but the height of the war occurred in 216 BCE with the Battle of Cannae. There, Hannibal used his superior cavalry to surround and attack the massive Roman army. Although they were outnumbered, Hannibal's military genius brought a victory to the Carthaginians. The Roman army was decimated, but this was not the end of the war. Once more, the Romans displayed their ability to adapt quickly. After employing the young military general Publius Cornelius Scipio (better known as Scipio Africanus today), Rome gained territories in Spain and Africa, forcing Carthage to leave Italy and defend their territory. In 203 BCE, Hannibal and Scipio clashed in Africa, and the Romans managed to make the Carthaginians retreat. More losses followed for Hannibal, and these eventually decided the outcome of the war. Carthage was reduced to only to its possessions in northern Africa, and Rome successfully conquered Spain.

The Third Punic War (149-146 BCE) was the final conflict between Rome and Carthage. It occurred because Carthage broke one of the conditions of the peace that had been implemented after the Second Punic War. Namely, Carthage wasn't allowed to wage war without Rome's permission unless it was to defend their territories. Carthage was attacked by the Numidians, but it ventured into their territory to fight. This was reason enough for Rome to declare a new war with Carthage. The truth is that Rome sought any reason to end Carthage's presence in the Mediterranean and take over control of the whole trade. It was the speculations of Senator Cato the Elder and his supporters that convinced the Roman Senate to proclaim this final war. The Roman army was sent to North Africa, where the entirety of the war happened. Rome decided to give the command of the army to Scipio Aemilianus (also known as Scipio the Younger). In 146 BCE, Aemilianus decided to launch a final attack on Carthage. His army managed to break into the city and destroy the residential areas, pushing toward the city's citadel. The final conflict lasted for seven days. The massacre continued until the Carthaginians were forced to surrender. The ancient city of Carthage was obliterated, and the estimations are that only 50 000 citizens survived. These citizens were then sold into slavery. Around 650,000 Carthaginians were killed, both soldiers and civilians. Carthage was no more, and it would take another century for the Romans to rebuild the city. Northern Africa became a Roman province, with its new capital at Utica.

Italy and The Roman Empire

After the Punic Wars, Rome became immensely powerful. Alongside the Punic Wars, Rome fought with other Mediterranean kingdoms to impose absolute dominion in this part of the world. Their four wars against Macedonia, one against the Seleucid Empire, and the one against the Achaean League (a confederation of Greek city-states of Peloponnese) are generally known as the Macedonian

Wars (214-148 BCE). Rome won on all fronts, and in a military sense, it became an empire. However, it was politically still a republic, but that was about to change. In the meantime, the Germanic tribes of the north were on the move. In the late 2nd century, the Romans and the Germanic tribes of Cimbri, Teutons, and Ambrones clashed, as the migratory people endangered Italy itself. They came from the Jutland Peninsula (north of modern-day Germany and part of continental Denmark), and they posed the biggest threat Rome had seen since the Punic Wars. The conflict was named the Cimbrian War (113-101 BCE) after the tribe Cimbri, and it was the inspiration for the military and political reforms that occurred in Rome at the time. The final organization of Roman legions was introduced by the military commander and consul Gaius Marius. He created the army that would last for many centuries, a force that would enter the history books as one of the most disciplined and successful armies in the world.

One person who greatly benefited from the Marian reforms was the nephew of Gaius Marius, Gaius Julius Caesar (100-44 BCE). The newly organized troops were extremely loyal to their leaders, and without their support, Caesar would never have been able to take over Rome and start the social reforms that would lead to the creation of the Roman Empire. In Rome, the middle of the 1st century was marked by bloody conflicts between political enemies, namely Caesar and Gnaeus Pompeius Magnus (better known as Pompey). At first, they were friends and allies, and each won important victories (Caesar in France against the Gauls and Pompey in today's Turkey against Mithridates VI of Pontus). Together with Marcus Licinius Crassus, they formed the First Triumvirate, which would bring about reforms to Rome, whose people were suffering due to the land grabbing by the rich. But the three of them became too powerful and wealthy, and it was only a matter of time before they would turn against each other. This occurred in 49 BCE, and by the end of 48, Pompey had been assassinated in Egypt. Caesar was left alone with all the powers of an emperor. Some scholars regard him as the first emperor of Rome, as he was given such privileges that he was equal to the gods. But his title was "dictator," which meant he would hold power over Rome until the immediate threat to the republic was over. Caesar had grandiose plans for Rome and its people, but he never lived long enough to fulfill them. On March 15th, 44 BCE, he was assassinated. His assassins, the senators, claimed they did this for the liberty of Rome, as Caesar wielded tremendous power. He was closer to the kings of old, which Rome swore never to allow again, than to the dictator of the republic. However, liberty didn't follow Caesar's death. Instead, another ten years of civil war took place. The animosity between Mark Antony and Caesar's nephew Octavian led Rome into a new era. In 31 BCE, Octavian defeated Antony at Actium (northern Greece) and took the title Augustus, becoming the first emperor of Rome.

Octavian added the title Augustus (Venerable) to his name, and in history, he is remembered as Emperor Augustus. Although his successors would take the same title for themselves, none of them would be remembered by it. Augustus ruled for forty years, which is marked as the height of Roman history. Rome continued its expansionist politics, but it had no enemy powerful enough to pose a serious threat. These were the years of peace and prosperity, and the legions were stationed at the borders of the empire to secure its defense. These outer provinces were known as the imperial provinces, while the peaceful provinces inside the empire were the senatorial provinces. Peace reigned in the senatorial provinces, as they were not under immediate danger from outside enemies. They were also unlikely to rebel and try to gain independence from Rome. Italy, on the other hand, had a special status. Although peace ruled all over Italy, it wasn't considered a province. Italy was the motherland, and it was directly under the administration of the Roman Senate. All other provinces, imperial or senatorial, were ruled by a dedicated governor.

By the time Octavian became emperor, all peoples who lived in Italy were granted Roman citizenship. This gave them the right to not only vote but to take part in the active political life of the empire. Although women were granted citizenship too, they were not allowed to vote. This was because the Roman Empire was not yet what we today consider an empire. Augustus held ultimate power, but the Senate still operated under him, and they were still led by the policies of the republic. The Romans couldn't imagine being ruled by only one man, and even if that was the reality, they needed this pretense of the power being shared between the emperor and the Senate.

The borders of Italy changed during the rule of Augustus, as he extended Roman citizenship to the peoples of the Aosta Valley. He also included the western and northern Alps within the Italian borders, so its western border was now at the Varus River. The cities within Italy had different political status; while some outright belonged to Rome, others had limited autonomy. The third type of Italian cities were Roman colonies. For easier administration, Augustus divided Italy into eleven different regions. Some were completely new, while others followed the old borders of regions, such as Samnium, Umbria, and Liguria. Augustus and his successors gave Italy priority when it came to the construction of roads and public buildings. These building projects brought economic prosperity to the Apennine Peninsula, which was now able to export goods with ease. Roads connected the Italian mainland with the shores and harbors from where the ships took various agricultural and handcrafted goods for sale across the Mediterranean Sea.

But it wasn't only the economy that grew. With peace and prosperity, it was natural for people to grow exponentially. Augustus demanded a census to be taken on three different occasions, but the results are inconclusive as of today. We don't know if all Roman citizens were counted or only adult male citizens; perhaps only the politically active adult male citizens were counted. However, modern scholars estimate that the people of mainland Italy during the 1st

century CE grew anywhere between six million and fourteen million. With this growth of citizens, arts and literature flourished in Italy. Wealthy citizens invested in the arts, which included the emperor himself. But art wasn't appreciated only for its beauty and as a means to enrich the people's culture. It played a political role in bringing the propaganda of the ruling classes to the common people and of Augustus to his subjects. The emperor ordered the famous epic *Aeneid*, written by Virgil, in which the Augustus's ancestry is explained to suit the imperial narrative. Emperors were now seen as the direct descendants of heroes of the Trojan War and Romulus and Remus, the founders of Rome. The conflict between Carthage and Rome was also justified in the *Aeneid*. Aeneas refused the love of the mythic Queen Dido of Carthage. This legendary refusal laid the basis for the conflict that had occurred, even though the myth sprouted after it. It was nothing more than propaganda that served to drive the imperial machinery of Rome.

The idea of Italy as a united nation was born during the rule of Augustus. Maybe it was the original idea of Virgil, who symbolically united Rome and Italia, a goddess (who, at the time, was known as Cybele, the Great Mother), through his works. However, Virgil's Italy was different from Augustus's vision. The emperor used this idea for his political purposes. For Virgil, Italy was an idea of a united nation, no matter how diverse. For Augustus, Italy was a territory that swore allegiance to him. The emperor couldn't see past his ambitions, and since he regarded Italy as an administrative convenience, his division of the regions carefully followed old ethnic boundaries. The common citizens, unlike the ruling class, had a larger appreciation of Italy, which they considered their homeland. There is written evidence that soldiers would often claim two homelands: Italy and the cities where they were born.

However, Italy wasn't yet united, although the sense of unity did exist. It wasn't a federation of different Italic territories but a political union of administrative units. As such, political ideas could be born anywhere, but eventually, they would lead to the center of the empire, to Rome. This city wasn't simply a city. It was the beginning and the end of all imperial matters. Rome was the center of the universe for the people of Italy, and they couldn't separate their identities from it. One could live in the new colonial city of Florentia (Florence) and still call himself Roman. This dual sense of patriotism was a product of various treaties and alliances the Italic peoples had conducted between themselves. The people had a greater sense of unity, and the nation of Italy could have been born then. But the idea was suppressed by the imperial needs of the upper class, who moved the transformation of the republic into an empire.

The powerful Roman Empire met its height with Augustus, and his successors were more or less capable of preserving those heights. The megalomania, corruption, and degeneracy of the Roman rulers came as a consequence of the vast influence and power of Rome. The imperial leadership started degrading, and incapable rulers such as Caligula, Nero, and Antoninus Pius made murder, destruction, and corruption a part of normal life. Nevertheless, the Roman Empire continued to thrive, and it encouraged free trade and justice; even the first alimony was created during this time, which was to secure the well-being of orphaned and poor children. The whole of Italy was a country of young people, and the Romans understood the importance of children. For them, children didn't only secure the longevity of the family name, but they were also the empire's future. Roman citizens typically died at the age of thirty-five. This was due to the high death rates of abled men who fought wars, but it was also due to high childhood mortality rates. Children rarely lived to see their fifteenth birthday, and knowing this, the Romans cared for their future generations.

The Roman Empire transformed over the centuries, and after Nero's rule, military generals emerged as emperors. They were of lower social classes, and they could be the sons of successful military generals, grandsons of simple sheepherders, or local prostitutes.

However, some of them proved to be capable, if not the best rulers, of the empire. Trajan (98–117 CE) and Hadrian (117–138) weren't even born in Italy. They came from the Spanish provinces, while their successors were Gauls, Thracians, or Illyrians.

Although the Roman Empire warred constantly, Italy and many of the senatorial provinces enjoyed continuous peace. The cities of Italy didn't need high walls, as the conflicts never reached them. The 1st, 2nd, and 3rd centuries and a big portion of the 4th century were times of relative peace. The empire reached its greatest size during the reign of Emperor Trajan. It spread from Britannia in the north to northern Africa, together with Egypt, in the south. The west occupied all the territories of the Iberian Peninsula and France, and to the east, it stretched all the way to Mesopotamia and Assyria. The Roman Empire was so huge that Emperor Diocletian (284–305) saw the wisdom in sharing the rule with others to take firmer control over all the territories under their protection. He devised a tetrarchy, a system of government in which four emperors shared the rule between themselves. The empire was split into two major territories: the West and the East. Each of them was split again into northern and southern halves, which were ruled by different individuals. But there was only one emperor above all: Diocletian.

The tetrarchy didn't live long, as it was doomed to fail with the death of its founder. Each of the remaining emperors saw an opportunity to impose their own dominance, and a series of conflicts followed. Only one ruler emerged as the final victor: Constantine the Great. He moved the capital from Rome to his newly founded city of Constantinople. There, he proclaimed Christianity as the official faith of the empire, and with that move, Italy entered a new phase of history.

Chapter 4 – Barbarian and Byzantine Italy

Defining the history of Italy is a rather difficult task. As we saw, for ancient Romans, Italia was a concept where everyone was united as Roman citizens. But this concept was quickly suppressed by the imperial administrative needs, and Italia became a geographical unit, a peninsula inhabited by various peoples of various statuses. During Late Antiquity, Rome spread its influence to the East, where a new empire emerged. Even though it never belonged to Italy proper (the Italian Peninsula), the Byzantine Empire was still an integral part. During the classical period, Italy was part of the Roman Empire. Late Antiquity and the early medieval period would see the peninsula ruled by outsiders, those who were once its subjects.

In 330, Constantine the Great moved the capital of the Roman Empire from Rome to his newly founded city, Constantinople, which was named after him. But this wasn't the only change within the empire. The official religion was now Christianity, and the new emperors were pious individuals whose strength lay in their faith. The Roman Empire began to resemble the kingdoms of medieval times. Rome remained an important center, as the religious leaders continued to see this city as a sacred place. In Rome, the first pope,

Saint Peter (Peter the Apostle), was crucified for simply being a Christian. While the new Roman emperors tried to move the main Christian see to Constantinople, the clergy resisted. Finally, the decision was made that the pope would remain in Rome and that a patriarch would be installed in Constantinople. This division of Christian leaders would present the empire with many problems. Each sees, the one in Rome and the one in Constantinople, would argue its right to be the supreme leader of the faith.

But the real split between the East and West occurred when Emperor Theodosius I (r. 379-395) wanted both of his sons to inherit the throne. Arcadius (r. 383-408) would be the emperor in the East, and Honorius (r. 393-423) would rule in the West. But the West had been weakened since the time of Constantine the Great. Although not intentionally, Constantine ignored the West. By moving the capital to Constantinople, he brought the attention of traders and investors to the East. Thus, the West was abandoned economically, and it staggered behind the East when it came to development. Constantinople needed new roads and building projects to enhance the new capital, and the taxes to pay for this was raised in the West. This economic gap between the East and West influenced the decline of the Western Roman Empire.

The East, on the other hand, thrived and prospered. Constantinople was one of the richest and strongest cities in the world. It is no wonder that the enemies of the empire ignored the East and tore apart the West like wolves. Italy was particularly interesting to the invading Huns, Goths, and Vandals. Honorius's rule may have been long, but he was unable to defend his empire, let alone return it to its previous glory. Since Diocletian, the Western Roman Empire had been governed from Mediolanum (today's Milan), while Rome became a religious and ceremonial center. Honorius moved the western capital from Mediolanum to Ravenna because it was better connected, by sea, with the Eastern Roman Empire, where his brother reigned. During the rule of Honorius, Rome was sacked. King Alaric

(r. 395-410) of the Visigoths bypassed Ravenna and led his army straight to Rome in 410. At the time, Rome already bore the title of "Eternal City," and as the spiritual center of the western half of the empire, it was still very rich and popular. No one could imagine the Eternal City falling into barbarian hands. However, the lack of a defensive army made it an attractive target. The sack of Rome, the first one after almost 800 years, is today regarded as a turning point in history. After this point, the fall of the Western Roman Empire was imminent.

But Italy itself was invaded ten years before the sacking of Rome. It wasn't the intention of the Visigoths to conquer the people of Italy. They just needed a new territory where they could settle, work the land, and live their everyday lives. To them, Italy was a territory that was good enough to support their increasing numbers. Even the sack of Rome was done in such a way that the people realized they were not being conquered. Alaric and his soldiers took the riches they needed and left the city in peace. Christian legends tell us how the Visigoths were touched by God and left without destroying any major buildings or killing civilians. But these legends are just that. The historical truth is different. Although there was no major destruction of the buildings (only two basilicas were burned) and no mass killing of the city's inhabitants, many died trying to save their riches. Others were tortured, raped, or sold into slavery.

After the sacking of Rome, Alaric led his army to southern Italy, and they even tried to cross the Mediterranean Sea and reach North Africa, but the short illness and death of their king prevented them. After Alaric's death, the Visigoths returned to their kingdom in southern France and even became allies with the Western Roman Empire, helping in its defense against the Huns. Nevertheless, their move against the empire in the early 400s and their rampage in Italy only served to continue the downfall of the Western Roman Empire.

History teaches us that Rome fell due to the barbarian attacks, and we are prone to imagine one great battle between the imperial army and the savage Germanic tribes, in which the Western Roman Empire was obliterated. But the end of the Western Roman Empire did not occur overnight. It wasn't a single event that brought the once-great Roman legions to their knees. It was a series of events, which took place over a period of time. The Visigoths were not the only ones attacking Italy and other provinces of the empire. The Vandals sacked Rome in 455, and although their name bears a negative connotation today, they didn't burn any of the buildings, and they spared its citizens. Their sack of the city was even more peaceful than that of Alaric's army. The Christian monks and priests wrote about the mercy the Vandals showed to Rome, but imperial propaganda demanded that this tribe be displayed in the worst possible way. Roman historians, who were faithful servants of imperial propaganda, did a good job of describing the Vandals as savages, whose only purpose was to loot, pillage, and destroy. It is no wonder the Romans despised the Vandals. They did more than sack their Eternal City, which showed how weak the empire was. Even earlier, in around 435, the Vandals conquered the Roman provinces in northern Africa, where they founded their own kingdom, which they successfully ruled for almost a century. They added to the misery of the Western Roman Empire, bringing its final fall ever closer.

Odoacer (r. 476-493) and Theodoric the Great (r. 493-526)

Historians argue over who was the last emperor of the Western Roman Empire. While some support the theory that it was Julius Nepos (r. 474-475), others are in favor of Romulus Augustulus (r. 475-476), who was still a child and had no support of the Eastern Roman Empire. Romulus was a puppet of his ambitious father, Orestes, the military commander in the court of Julius Nepos. Orestes raised a rebellion against Nepos, and after defeating him, he sent Nepos into exile. However, placing his underaged son as the new emperor didn't bring Orestes the new alliances he needed to fight off the rebellion of the barbarian tribes already settled in Italy. Under the leadership of a military officer named Odoacer, they easily defeated

Orestes in 476, exiled his son, and started a new era in Italy. Odoacer was the first king of Italy, even though he was a barbarian.

The ethnicity of Odoacer remains a mystery. Contemporary writers and historians are divided in the way they address him. While some claim he was a Goth, others thought he came with Attila the Hun's multinational army. Modern historians are inclined to think that Odoacer had origins among the eastern Germanic tribes, but conclusive evidence eludes us. Nothing is known of Odoacer's early life except that he wasn't born in Italy. He joined the Roman army, and by 470, he became the officer of the *foederati* (barbarians fighting on Rome's side, who were bound by a treaty), which consisted of various Germanic tribes. Once Orestes raised his son to the throne of the Western Roman Empire, the *foederati* were the first to be suspicious of his intentions and capabilities, as both father and son had no support of the Eastern Roman Empire, which continued to regard Julius Nepos as the legitimate emperor in the West. However, the *foederati* didn't act on their suspicions. They approached Orestes and asked him for land of their own within Italy, where they could settle. They thought it would be payment for their military services, but Orestes refused them. Having nothing else to lose, the *foederati* turned to Odoacer, who led them in a rebellion.

The rebellion soon grew into an invasion, and the armies of Odoacer swelled with barbarian tribes. Orestes mounted the defense, but since he had no allies, he failed to defend the throne. Odoacer killed Orestes at Placentia (today's Piacenza), but he spared the sixteen-year-old emperor. History lost track of Romulus after this point, and no one knows what became of him. On September 4th, 476, the Senate in Ravenna persuaded Romulus Augustulus to abdicate in favor of the invaders. This date is officially considered to be when the fall of the Western Roman Empire took place. However, as seen before, the imperial West had been collapsing slowly since the reign of Constantine the Great.

There was no one yet on the imperial throne in Ravenna, as Julius Nepos continued to claim he was the legitimate ruler in the West. He organized his new court in Dalmatia, where he even received the officials of the Eastern Roman Empire who still supported him. But only four years later, Nepos was assassinated while planning the return of Italy under his reign. Odoacer took the opportunity and invaded Dalmatia after his death.

Odoacer ruled Italy as its king from 476, and it seems he had the support and loyalty of the Roman Senate. He politically and militarily strengthened his kingdom, keeping good relations with the Church. Italy began to recover under his rule, and it seemed that political and economic stability was returning to the West. But in Constantinople, Flavius Zeno (r. 476-491) ruled, and he considered Odoacer to be his enemy, even though he recognized his legitimacy after the death of Nepos. Zeno persuaded Theodoric, the commander of the Eastern Roman forces and the ruler of the Ostrogoths, a tribe that often rebelled against Constantinople, to instead attack Odoacer in Italy.

In 488, Italy became the battlefield where Theodoric and Odoacer fought for dominance. Theodoric won some of the initial battles, but his progress was stopped, and he even lost a battle at Faenza in 490. For years, the conflict continued, and both of the leaders had their victories and losses. But when Theodoric managed to take Ravenna in 493, Odoacer realized how formidable his enemy was. Instead of continuing the fight, he signed an agreement of joint rulership. This way, they would stop the conflict from ravaging Italy, even though their personal ambitions were not satisfied. Theodoric proved to be too ambitious to accept a joint rule. During his coronation celebration in Ravenna, the new king pulled out his sword and personally killed Odoacer. His man took it as a sign, and all of Odoacer's men were slaughtered. Theodoric secured his sole rule over Italy through this bloody betrayal.

But it wasn't only the personal desire to rule that pushed Theodoric into attacking Italy. He was the leader of the Ostrogoths, and he needed a place where he could settle his people. Since he served the Eastern Roman Empire, he hoped Zeno would provide him with land as a reward. But Zeno declined to do this, and the animosity between the two grew. It is no wonder Theodoric often rebelled against Zeno. Now, as the king of Italy, he needed to overcome another problem. His Amal tribe counted only 40,000 people, and he was afraid that if he dispersed them through Italy, the tribe would disappear. Instead, he decided to settle the Amals around Pavia and Ravenna, keeping them all together.

Theodoric didn't only conquer the land; he conquered its people too. The devastation after years of conflict was so immense that it threatened to cause a famine among both the old and new settlers. Some areas went through heavy deforestation, as the army needed timber for constructing siege weapons. Without trees to serve as protection, many fertile fields turned into swamps. Theodoric ordered the drainage of these waters and new trees to be planted. He drilled wells in the areas that lacked rain and constructed irrigation canals to supply dry fields with water. The people he ruled were both Gothic and Roman, and as the king, he made no difference between them. He reorganized the laws so that all peoples of the Italian Peninsula would be treated equally. By the time Theodoric managed to conquer Italy and kill Odoacer, Zeno had died. The Eastern Roman Empire had a new ruler, Anastasius I Dicorus (r. 491–518), who accepted the new king of Italy and gave Theodoric and his successors legitimacy.

Theodoric was illiterate, but he encouraged education among his people and in his court. He gathered philosophers from around the world, as well as artists and religious figures. Theodoric cared for poorer people by making laws through which they would get free corn rations each year. He also rebuilt destroyed aqueducts, old Roman roads, and some prominent buildings, which opened up jobs for the less fortunate. He kept good relations with his neighbors by making alliances through marriages. He married the sister of the Frankish king and gave his daughters to the kings of the Visigoths and Burgundians. Through these marriages, Theodoric hoped to create one big kingdom that would unite the Gothic people of Europe. Those people who the Romans called barbarians were now emerging to rule the known world.

But Theodoric wasn't able to keep the peace between the European kingdoms. Although he had good relations with both the Franks and the Visigoths, he couldn't keep them from fighting each other. Soon, the Burgundians joined the conflict, and Theodoric's kingdom of Ostrogoths in Italy was endangered when his own son-in-law, Sigismund of Burgundy, attacked the Italian shores. Theodoric's opportunity to strengthen his kingdom came when the Visigothic prince Eutharic died in 522. He was married to Theodoric's daughter Amalasuntha, and together, they had a son named Athalaric. Since Theodoric never had a son, he proclaimed his grandson, Athalaric, to be his successor. Because the young boy was the Visigothic prince and the heir to the Ostrogothic throne, the kingdoms were united. During the height of Theodoric's rule (523), the Ostrogothic kingdom consisted of the territories in the Italian Peninsula, Dalmatia and Pannonia to the east, and Mediterranean France and the whole Iberian Peninsula to the west.

Up until this point, Theodoric was in good relations with all Christian churches within his kingdom. He belonged to Arian Christianity, but he was more than willing to tolerate the Trinitarians of Eastern Christianity. After all, good relations with Constantinople was important. The main difference between these two sects has to do with Jesus Christ. While Arians believe he was an individual who was different from his Heavenly Father, Trinitarians believed that Jesus was the same with God and the Holy Spirit. Today, the major Christian sects are unified in the opinion that Arianism is heresy, but in the early medieval period, it was one of many legitimate teachings. This doesn't mean that rulers tolerated all teachings. In

Constantinople, the new emperor, Justin I (r. 518–527), and his successor, Justinian I (527–565), were avid religion fighters. They belonged to the Trinitarians, and they were set on expelling all Arians from Constantinople and the Eastern Roman Empire. Theodoric, in response, changed his tolerance policy and started expelling all the Trinitarians from his Italian kingdom. Naturally, this led to tension between the court in Ravenna and the one in Constantinople.

It was probably this tension that doomed his successors. When Theodoric died in 526, the thirty years of peace and stability were over. He was succeeded, as planned, by his grandson, Athalaric. But he was still just a young boy, so his mother, Amalasuntha, became his regent. The untimely death of her son in 534 prompted Amalasuntha to proclaim herself a queen, and she ruled briefly from 534 until 535. However, she could not get the approval of Constantinople. In fact, Emperor Justinian I ignored her completely. Since her position on the throne was insecure, she decided to invite her cousin, Theodahad, to rule jointly with her. Unfortunately, Theodahad was ambitious, and he saw this invitation as an opportunity to take the Ostrogothic Kingdom for himself. As soon as he had the opportunity, he arrested Amalasuntha and exiled her just so he could later order her death.

But this wasn't the end of the dynastic troubles in the Kingdom of the Ostrogoths. Amalasuntha's son-in-law, Vitiges, rose to avenge her. He defeated Theodahad and took the throne of Italy, becoming the king in 536. But he didn't rule for long. In 540, Belisarius, a military commander of the Byzantine Empire, attacked Italy, defeated Vitiges, and claimed the whole peninsula for Emperor Justinian I. Italy was reunited with what was left of the Roman Empire.

The Gothic Wars (535–554)

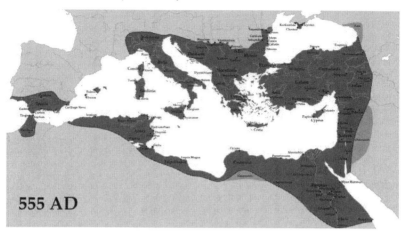

555 AD

Territories controlled by Emperor Justinian

https://en.wikipedia.org/wiki/Byzantine_Empire#/media/File;Justinian555AD.png

When Justinian became the emperor of the Eastern Roman Empire, he greatly desired to retrieve the former western possessions and place them under his control. He was ambitious and wanted Hispania and Britannia back under Roman influence, but his first priorities had to be Africa, which was the main grain supplier, and Italy, which was the cradle of the Roman civilization. Justinian wasn't a warrior himself, but he knew he could rely on the military genius of his commander, Belisarius. His first task was to wrestle northern Africa from the Vandals, who had occupied it for almost a whole century. Although Justinian dreamed about reuniting the empire, he wasn't willing to invest funds in military expeditions that would bring him closer to his dream. Instead, he equipped Belisarius with only a small fleet and a few legions. But Belisarius's commitment to his task was tremendous, and he managed to fulfill it against all odds. Underequipped and with a small army, Belisarius managed to bring North Africa back to what was left of the Roman Empire.

Belisarius's success was celebrated in Constantinople, and Justinian even organized a triumph for his military general, the first one for a non-emperor since the days of Tiberius's rule. The next step was to return Italy and Dalmatia to its rightful owner. For decades, they had been ruled by the Ostrogoths. Justinian not only wanted to return Italy back into the empire's fold, but he also wanted to deal with the heretics, as the Ostrogoths believed in Arianism. This time, he granted Belisarius a larger army and sent him on a mission to not only conquer the territories but also liberate the souls who suffered religious oppression under the Arian rulers.

The dynastic troubles among the Ostrogothic rulers of Italy made Belisarius's task even easier. The whole country was in dismay, and they were not certain to whom they owed their allegiance. The Ostrogothic army was divided, and during the early years of the campaign, which began in 535, Belisarius took Dalmatia and Sicily. In 536, Belisarius crossed the Adriatic Sea and entered the territory of Italy. After this initial victory, he decided to march directly to Rome. But there was no serious opposition or defense of the Eternal City, and the Eastern Roman army entered it in December that same year.

Justinian sent reinforcements from Constantinople, which ravaged the Italian shores while Belisarius continued the siege of Rome. The new king of the Ostrogoths, Vitiges, had to abandon Rome once the army of Huns, which was sent by Justinian, cut off their access to supplies. Over the next few years, the cities of Italy fell to the Eastern Roman army. But Ravenna, the capital, proved to be a challenge for Belisarius. To conquer it, Belisarius had to move the troops from Dalmatia and cut off the sea supply of the city, but even then, he was unable to take it.

Justinian sent a proposal to Vitiges to split the rule over Italy. The Goths would get the territories north of the Po River, while the rest of the peninsula would be a Byzantine possession under the direct rule of Constantinople. Belisarius believed he could achieve more and bring all of Italy to Justinian, so he refused to sign the treaty, which gave Vitiges the impression that Belisarius wished to rule Italy by himself. Even though this wasn't the impression Belisarius wanted to give, Vitiges saw an opportunity, and he offered to make Belisarius the

Western Roman emperor in return for more territories. Belisarius accepted the offer of the Gothic king, although he had no intention of betraying Emperor Justinian. By agreeing to Vitiges's deal, Belisarius was able to enter Ravenna in peace and capture the capital from inside. Almost all of Italy was under Byzantine rule. Only the territories in the north remained under the Ostrogoths.

After these dealings, Justinian was suspicious of his military commander, and he recalled him back to Constantinople to prevent him from becoming the western emperor. This move proved to be disastrous. With Belisarius gone, the Goths of the north became courageous enough to try retrieving their Italic territories. The Goths reorganized and rekindled the war with the Eastern Roman Empire. What could have been a brief conquest of the Italian Peninsula turned into twelve more years of war. Belisarius took Vitiges to Constantinople, where he was to sign the treaty directly under the supervision of Emperor Justinian and become his prisoner. The Goths who had remained in Italy to fight needed a new leader. They chose Baduila, who would be later known as Totila (r. 541–552), as their new monarch. The new Gothic king set out to do something Justinian never bothered to do: gain the trust of the Roman people of Italy.

When Justinian sent Belisarius to reconquer Italy, the Italic Romans didn't care to join his army. They were indifferent to the war between the Goths and Constantinople. For them, life continued, no matter who ruled. Baduila understood the importance of having the support of all the peoples of Italy, not just the Goths. It wasn't difficult to turn these people against Constantinople, as the emperor made them pay a "liberation tax." Even though Italy was devastated by the war, Justinian implemented additional taxation on its people to regain the money that had been lost in the war effort. Baduila promised equal taxes for all and the freedom to continue their labors undisturbed if they joined his efforts to return the Ostrogothic Kingdom in Italy. He even accepted the deflectors of the Eastern

Roman army, promising them better treatment. And finally, he offered slaves a place in his army and a promise they would never be returned to their masters.

Justinian again sent Belisarius, this time allowing him to take only 4,000 troops to Italy. This wasn't enough, as King Totila's army included all the Ostrogoths and the Romans of Italy. Totila had already taken Naples (543) when Belisarius arrived on the shores of Italy in 544. The Goths were already preparing to take Rome, and they sacked it in 546. The second siege of Rome occurred soon after, and Belisarius was successful in defending it. But in 549, the jealous Emperor Justinian recalled Belisarius to Constantinople again, where he retired from his military career. However, the Gothic Wars continued until, finally, General Narses managed to destroy the Ostrogothic Kingdom and bring Italy under Byzantine's fold in 554. After Constantinople finally had control over the peninsula, the Franks attacked from the north. The Byzantine Empire was financially drained by the wars, and keeping Italy seemed impossible. Justinian died in 565, and three years later, the Lombards came and conquered mainland Italy. Only Sicily and some cities in the south remained under direct Byzantine control.

Chapter 5 – The Kingdom of the Lombards and the Emergence of the Papal States

Territories controlled by the Lombards (in blue)
at the height of their power (749–756)

https://upload.wikimedia.org/wikipedia/commons/c/ce/Aistulf%27s_Italy-en.png

The Lombards were a Germanic tribe that invaded Italy after it was devastated by the Gothic Wars. Their origin can be traced to southern Scandinavia. However, sometime before the 1st century CE, they migrated to Pannonia, in what is today Hungary, but they also inhabited the territories of modern-day Austria and Slovakia, where they warred with other Germanic tribes. There is evidence that suggests the Lombards prospered in this part of Europe. They were ruled by a king as a united nation, and they defeated the Gepids (another Germanic tribe). King Alboin (r. 560–572) decided to take his people farther south to settle in Italy, which was heavily depopulated after the Gothic Wars. The previous war with the Gepids brought the rise of the Avars, who wanted dominance over the region. To fight the Avars, Albion married a Gepid princess so he could tie the Lombards and their previous enemy into an alliance against the Avars. But the Gepids were weakened to the point of extinction, and Alboin realized it was wiser to leave the area than to fight the mighty Avars.

Italy wasn't a random choice. A large number of Lombards had previously served the imperial army under the leadership of General Narses when he was fighting the last of the Gothic Wars. They had firsthand experience of what Italy was like, and they had witnessed its depopulation. It is possible that these soldiers suggested Alboin lead his people to Italy. However, some sources claim that it was Narses himself who invited them. Scholars don't know which source is telling the truth, but in 568, Alboin and his Lombards arrived in northern Italy.

When the Lombards first arrived in Italy, they conquered a great number of cities without much resistance from the imperial forces. Constantinople had no funds or manpower to hold its possessions in Italy and wage war in the East at the same time. This period of history is known as the Byzantine Dark Ages. The empire suffered various attacks, first from the Avars and Bulgars and then from the Persians of the Sassanid Empire. Byzantine simply had to pay less attention to

Italy. The Lombards took their opportunity, and by 572, they had conquered most of the Italian Peninsula. The only city in which resistance was organized was Pavia, and it took three years for Alboin to conquer it. The Lombard king set his capital in Verona and transferred it to Pavia once it was taken.

King Alboin is remembered for dividing Italy into thirty-six duchies. Each of them was governed by a duke, who was the only one with the power to report directly to the king. This division of Italy was a brilliant solution for the administration and bureaucracy of the kingdom, but it also had negative sides. The dukes were given too much executive power, and each duchy was at a different level of prosperity, depending on the capabilities of their dukes. While some regions prospered, other regions suffered poverty and famine due to the greedy and incapable men in power. The king's concentration was focused on the kingdom's borders because the Franks attempted invasions. Also, the Byzantine Empire continued its efforts to regain some of its previous holdings in Italy, and it often attacked the cities of the newly established Lombard Kingdom. This means the dukes led the internal affairs of the kingdom, and their rivalry resulted in a lack of unity between the regions.

From the beginning, the Lombard Kingdom was in a vulnerable state. Queen Rosamund, the wife of King Alboin, conspired to assassinate her husband. She convinced Alboin's foster brother, Helmichis, to kill him. She never forgave her husband for murdering her father, the king of the Gepids. Helmichis married Rosamund to secure his succession to the throne, but the assassination of the king had a devastating effect on the kingdom. The duchies lost whatever sense of unity they had, and the internal conflicts began. The Lombards lost the only king that was capable of holding them together, and the dukes started fighting each other. The kingdom was also threatened by the Franks, who were waiting for the perfect opportunity to strike the final blow.

The Byzantines still had some of their possessions in Italy, and Emperor Maurice (r. 582-602) made a real effort to retrieve even more Italian cities in 584. He founded the Exarchate of Ravenna, a political unit that would be the base for future actions in Italy. The exarchate grouped all of the duchies that were under Byzantine rule, such as Rome, Calabria, Perugia, Naples, and Venice. This unit was governed by an exarch, whose task was to organize the locals into an army. But the people of Italy had no intention of allowing the Byzantine emperor to rule them. They were tired of constant warfare and wished to see improvements, not more devastation. But it wasn't the people alone who were to blame for the failure of the exarchate. The pope in Rome was an unstable ally who had his own reasons to wish the Byzantines gone from Italy. In the beginning, the pope was the Byzantines' ally, but when the split between Orthodoxy and Catholicism, which was inspired by iconoclasm, occurred in 726, the pope was more on the side of the people and against the Exarchate of Ravenna. Eventually, the idea of the exarchate failed, with the exarchate dissolving in 751.

However, the imperial force of the exarchate prompted the Lombard dukes to stop fighting each other. They were forced to choose a leader who would unite them against their common enemy. In 584, they chose Authari as their new king. In 586, the Lombards defeated the Byzantine forces under the leadership of Exarch Smaragdus, but he soon lost some territories due to the constant attacks from Ravenna. At the same time, the Lombards suffered Frankish attacks. Hoping to create an alliance with them, Authari planned to marry the daughter of King Childebert II of the Franks. However, the negotiations between the two failed, and the Franks allied themselves with the Byzantine Empire against the Lombards. In 590, this alliance started a full-scale invasion of Italy, and in the same year, Authari died, though not in combat. He was probably poisoned by conspirators, and he was succeeded by Agilulf (r. 590-616), Duke of Turin.

The new king of the Lombards proved to be much more politically successful than his predecessor. He made peace and secured the borders with the Franks. Then he turned to reorganize the administration of the kingdom to suppress the dukes, who exercised too much power. Italy was now under the direct control of the king, not the dukes. This brought a new sense of unity, and the internal conflicts were reduced. At this point, the Byzantines had their hands filled with the Bulgars, Slavs, and Persians, so they had no time or resources to devote to the Italian problem. This brought relative peace to Italy, and Agilulf was able to concentrate on the internal problems. These were mostly of a religious nature. The Lombards were Arian Christians. On the other hand, the majority of the Roman population was Trinitarians. Even Agilulf's wife, Theodelinda, was a Roman Catholic, and she insisted on converting her husband. Agilulf agreed to do this to secure peace in his kingdom. He even baptized his sons as Catholics. Although Arianism was never banned from the Kingdom of the Lombards, the religious conflict between the two groups perished. Arian dukes were known for being patrons of Catholic shrines, and there was a persistent lack of religious debates or confrontations from this point on.

This religious peace and national unity caused the Lombards to adopt the material and spiritual culture of their fellow Roman inhabitants of the Italian peninsula. Their clothes, manners, and customs changed from being similar to those of the Franks and Goths to purely Roman. The leftovers of the Lombard pagan rituals slowly disappeared and were replaced by Catholicism, although those same pagan rituals could still be observed among the Franks. The Lombards started baptizing their children as Catholics, probably following the example of their king, and the new names they chose for their sons and daughters were all of Roman origin. When Agilulf died in 616, his queen ruled as the regent until 626, which was when their son, Adaloald, reached adulthood. But he was quickly deposed by Arioald (r. 626–636), his brother-in-law, who was an Arian. Arioald openly objected to Catholicism, and he reestablished Arianism among the Lombard elite. However, he only ruled for ten years and was mostly busy fighting the Avars. He didn't manage to ignite a true religious conflict between the Arians and Trinitarians.

After Arioald, Rothari came to power. He was considered one of the best Lombard kings. Under his rule, the Lombards resumed their fight against the Byzantine Empire, and they managed to expand their kingdom. Constantinople now had possession of only Rome and some minor coastal provinces. The north and the hinterlands of Italy were under the firm rule of the Lombards. Most of the southern provinces swore allegiance to the Lombard king, but some of the coastal cities resisted, as they were loyal to the Byzantine Empire. Rothari is known for issuing the first Lombard law, known as the *Edictum Rothari*, in 643. This new set of laws only applied to his Lombard subjects, meaning the Romans still lived under Roman law but within the Lombard jurisdiction. Even though he was an effective king who was loved by his people, Rothari had his share of political enemies. When he died, his son Rodoald came to power. However, the new king was immediately assassinated by his father's enemies.

The stability of the Lombard Kingdom was shaken. The political conflicts within the realm divided the rule between two individuals. One had his base in Milan, while the other one remained in Pavia. This divide would eventually grow into the obvious decline of the Lombard Kingdom. They did not only fight between themselves, but they also led a war against the invading Slavs, who were at their borders. In 712, Liutprand took the throne and managed to unite the nation. He ruled until 744, and he is often referred to as the greatest Lombard king since the rule of Alboin. Liutprand forged an alliance with the Franks, and with their help, he expanded the Kingdom of the Lombards beyond the territories that had been taken by Rothari. He is also remembered for the Donation of Sutri, the first agreement between the Lombards and the pope, which was signed in 728. Liutprand gave some of the cities in Latium to Pope Gregory II as a gift, probably to ensure the pope broke his allegiance to the Byzantine Empire. The papacy gained its first territories outside of the Duchy of Rome through the Donation of Sutri, a move that would ensure the rise of the Papal States.

After the death of Liutprand, a series of weak and incompetent kings followed, although some of them managed to expand their possessions. In 751, the Exarchate of Ravenna fell when the Lombards managed to kill the last Byzantine exarch, Eutychius. Some of the territories remained under Byzantine rule, and they were reorganized into the Catepanate of Italy, but the capital was moved to Bari. However, this territory would soon fall to the Saracens, and the Byzantine presence in Italy would be confined to a very small region in southern Italy. But that doesn't mean Byzantine would give up. In the 9th century, the effort to recapture Italy and Dalmatia was renewed with Emperor Basil I.

Pope Stephen II crowned Pepin the Short as the king of the Franks in 751 and granted him the title Protector of Rome. The king of the Franks was now bound into an alliance with the pope, and on his orders and under the pretense of defending the holy see, Pepin attacked northern Italy and conquered some of its regions in 756. The defeated Lombards were forced to retreat, as Pepin gifted the territories to the pope (known as the Donation of Pepin). The last king of the Lombards, Desiderius (r. 756-774), tried to make peace with the Franks by marrying his daughter to Prince Charlemagne, the future Frankish king. But Pope Stephen III opposed this marriage, which deepened the conflict between the Lombards and the papacy. Stephen even persuaded some of the Lombard dukes to leave the kingdom and join their forces with the Franks. Charlemagne was crowned as the king of the Franks by Pope Stephen III in 768 and was obliged to fight against the Lombards. But in order to do so, the Frankish king had to divorce Desiderius's daughter, which he gladly did so he could marry Hildegard of Swabia and create a new alliance. In 773, Charlemagne invaded Italy, and once he managed to defeat the Lombard resistance, he captured the capital of the kingdom, Pavia. Desiderata and his wife were exiled, but Charlemagne didn't want to disband the already functioning kingdom. He maintained its administration and laws, but he replaced the dukes with counts, basing the new governance of Italy on the Frankish model. Lombard's rule of Italy came to an end, but its people remained. Though they have been assimilated with the Romans, they are still a part of the Italian nation.

In 781, Charlemagne gifted even more territories to the pope, and parts of the territories of Ravenna, Pentapolis, Tuscany, Lombardy, and Corsica became the Papal States. The alliance between the Carolingian Frankish dynasty and the popes of Rome lasted for a very long time. Even though they had some differences and even conflicts, this alliance was fruitful for both sides. It truly began in 800 when Pope Leo III crowned Charlemagne as emperor and created the Roman Empire. Once again, there were two Roman emperors, one in the East and the other in the West. The adjective "Holy" was added later in 1157 when the West was ruled by Frederick I Barbarossa, King of Germany.

Even during the existence of the Holy Roman Empire, the Papal States thrived. They were not just territories united under a religious ruler. These were territories in which both ecclesiastical and secular power was in the hands of the pope. This power is known by the name "temporal power of the pope." The Papal States persisted through the Middle Ages, the Renaissance, and well into the modern era. But the citizens of these territories didn't necessarily want to be ruled by the pope. The rebellions and various political factions often brought about a decline in the quality of life, which, in turn, started another series of rebellions. At one point, Pope Clement V moved his court to Avignon in France. This city became the first and only Papal State outside of Italy. The Papal States ended around 1870, during the Napoleonic Wars, when the united Italian Army captured Rome. The pope refused to become the subject of the Kingdom of Italy, and he closed himself in the Vatican. Even today, the Holy See remains in the Vatican, which is located within Rome. In February 1929, the State of the Vatican City was officially recognized, and it remains the only surviving Papal State.

Chapter 6 – Italy's Place in the Holy Roman Empire

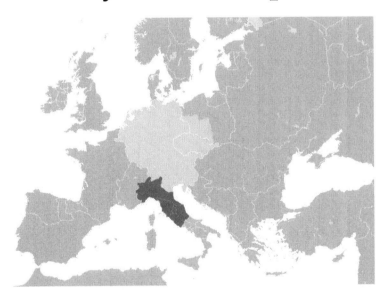

Italy within the Holy Roman Empire

https://en.wikipedia.org/wiki/Kingdom_of_Italy_(Holy_Roman_Empire)
#/media/File:Kingdom_of_Italy_1000.svg

Pope Leo III and Charlemagne returned the title of emperor to the West. But the territories they consecrated as an empire weren't yet a part of the Holy Roman Empire. Italy was part of the Carolingian

Empire, which was under Frankish dominion, but it wasn't annexed. Instead, Charlemagne proclaimed himself the king of the Lombards, admitting that Italy and Francia were separate kingdoms ruled by one king. The Lombards never really disappeared from Italy. The aristocratic families retreated to the south, where other Lombards still had control of Benevento. Here, the Lombard dukes ruled for the next 300 years.

When Emperor Lothair I died in 855, the Carolingian Empire was split between his three sons. Louis II was the eldest, and he gained the territories of Italy, which included all the lands in the north. The Italian kingdom spread southward to Rome, but it didn't include the pope's city. Farther to the south were the Lombards in Benevento and the possessions of the Byzantine Empire. Even though it was still part of the Carolingian Empire, Italy, once again, was regarded as a separate political territory with its own king. But after the death of Louis II, there was much confusion. Who should inherit Italy now? The two pretenders for the Italian throne were Charles the Bald of West Francia, which is today's France, and Charles the Fat of East Francia, a territory that corresponds with today's Germany. Charles the Fat took the throne of Italy in 880 and made it his permanent residency until the end of his rule in 887.

The following decades in Italy saw many claimants to the throne. Italy briefly became an independent kingdom when the local noble families of Spoleto and Friuli argued over the crown. Even intervention from outside didn't restore order within the Italian borders. Between 888 and 962, there were at least eleven individuals who claimed to be kings of Italy. The stability didn't return to Italy until the middle of the 10th century when Otto of Germany claimed the throne. He was married to Adelaide, who was the daughter and wife of three previous Italian kings. Otto followed the example of Charlemagne; instead of annexing the kingdom, he took the crown, naming himself the king of the Lombards. In 962, Pope John XII crowned him emperor, which started the German rule over Italy.

Over the next three centuries, three separate German dynasties would rule: Saxon, Salian, and Swabian (Hohenstaufen).

The German emperors had a very complex role. They were elected by the German princes and would be crowned as the kings of Germany. At that moment, they would also become the kings of the Romans. Then they were obliged to cross the Alps and enter Pavia, where they would be crowned as the kings of the Lombards. And finally, they would visit Rome, where the pope would crown them as the emperors of the Roman Empire. By traveling the length and breadth of his territory in this way, the emperor realized the size of his empire. It stretched from the Baltic and the North Seas to the Adriatic and the Tyrrhenian to the south. Since he ruled over such a vast area, Italy was often neglected. Even though the emperor had his institutions and supporters in the Italian Peninsula, the lack of his presence encouraged the magnates to plot against him. But no serious threat to the integrity of the empire happened during this time. The cities and agriculture prospered, and the number of people in Italy had doubled since the depopulation of the Gothic Wars. The people enjoyed relative wealth, and the absence of a ruler inspired them to try to take control of their city's affairs. Communes rose, and in them, leaders were chosen, and they had the power to run the courts and raise an army. The emperors were too busy fighting wars outside of their borders, so the communes slowly gained a certain level of autonomy. By the 11th century, the Lombard and Tuscan cities had autonomy in everything but name.

In 1155, a new emperor came to the throne. His name was Frederick Barbarossa (r. 1155-1190). He was determined to change the situation in Italy and put a stop to the communes and their strive for autonomy. He considered himself to be the successor of Caesar, and he even claimed to be equivalent to the Augustus of the ancient Roman Empire. In his eyes, the kings of England and France were inferior, let alone the kings of smaller European nations, such as Sweden or Galicia. He planned to get rid of the local rulers and communes in Italy and install his own men as the city officials. He also wanted to collect taxes on Italian goods, as well as the tolls and customs. His predecessors had allowed local magnates to rise to power and collect these taxes for themselves.

Barbarossa didn't have much trouble returning most of the Italian cities to the empire's fold, but Milan was resistant. To subjugate it, he needed to invade Italy no less than six times. He did it under the pretense of saving those cities that had remained loyal to the empire from the invading Milanese. In 1162, he captured Milan and destroyed the city. On his way was the town of Crema, which was a Milanese ally, and it was also destroyed. Barbarossa was so brutal during his invasions in Italy that, to defend themselves, sixteen cities formed an alliance named the Lombard League. In 1176, during the Battle of Legnano (near Milan), the League won a major victory against the emperor. But a treaty wasn't signed until 1183 when Barbarossa finally agreed that the communes should have the right to elect their own leaders and administer the territories under their laws. Barbarossa died, drowning himself in a river, while on his way to join the Third Crusade seven years later. His grandson, Frederick II (r. 1220–1250), tried to repeat Barbarossa's efforts in Italy, but he was equally unsuccessful.

During the conflict of the communes and Barbarossa, the papacy was, surprisingly, on the side of the Lombard League. The pope even called on the princes of Germany and France to abandon their emperor and join the holy cause. The conflict arose when Barbarossa refused to support Alexander III as pope and instead gave his support to antipope Victor IV. At the time, Italy wasn't only in conflict with Emperor Barbarossa. There were conflicts between the communes themselves, which arose when some supported the pope while others believed in the imperial power. The papal supporters were known as Guelphs, and their opponents, the supporters of the empire, were Ghibellines. But in reality, the fight between the Guelphs and

Ghibellines was motivated more by local factors than by their loyalties to the emperor or pope.

Normans in Sicily

While the medieval period in northern Italy saw the rise of the Holy Roman Empire and the clash of its emperors and the popes, the south was going through something completely different. In fact, during the Middle Ages, there were two Italies. In the north, the people and cities prospered under imperial rule and later during the individual communes, which were always in touch with the rest of Europe through the passes of the Alps. In the south, the Byzantines, Greeks, and Arabs relied on the Mediterranean Sea and its trade with distant lands. Italy was divided, and the two halves of the same peninsula looked like two different worlds. But this doesn't mean that the two halves of Italy weren't interested in each other. In the south, conflicts between the pope and the emperor would rise, especially when it came to the status of the Kingdom of Sicily.

From the late 10th century to well into the 12th century, the Normans conquered southern Italy. At first, the Normans came to Italy as mercenaries, and they were hired by the Lombard and Byzantine rulers. Since wars were expensive, rulers often had no money to pay the hired army. Instead, they rewarded them land within their domain as a reward for their service. But within only fifty years after their initial arrival, the Normans owned so much land in southern Italy that they had them organized into fiefdoms and soon united in demanding complete independence from those who had hired them in the first place. But it took time and many battles for the Normans to acquire their independence. Even though it is called the Norman conquest of Italy, there wasn't one decisive battle that granted them this victory. The conquest was a result of decades of dedication, conflicts, and persistence. Even Pope Leo IX feared the Normans would become too powerful in the south, and he organized an army to fight them off. However, this pope was defeated and captured by Robert Guiscard in 1053. The two made a deal that if

Robert Guiscard recognized papal sovereignty over the south, he would be given the title "Duke of Apulia and Calabria and future Duke of Sicily." The adjective "future" was removed in 1061 when Robert invaded Sicily.

Robert Guiscard soon turned his attention to the Byzantine territories, where he conquered Bari in 1071, and then he defeated the Arabs of Sicily. In 1072, Palermo was his possession, and by 1090, the island of Sicily was defeated. His nephew, Roger II, succeeded him and united the Norman territories of Sicily and the southern mainland of the Italian Peninsula, creating the Kingdom of Sicily and the Hauteville dynasty. It is imperative to understand that the name of the kingdom, even though it was borrowed from the island of Sicily, also applied to other territories ruled by the Normans. The kingdom included the Maltese archipelago, Sicily, and the Duchy of Apulia and Calabria. In 1146, Roger II expanded his kingdom to include African territories by capturing the region that was known as Ifriqiya (parts of today's Libya, Algeria, and Tunis).

The first king of Sicily understood very well that he ruled over a very diverse people. Among them were Byzantines, Latins, Greeks, Arabs, Jews, and other minorities of the Mediterranean world. Because of this, he refused to join the Crusades so he could keep the peace between his subjects. Roger II insisted that all laws and customs of his subjects should be equally respected, and he promoted religious freedom throughout his kingdom. Under his rule, southern Italy flourished, and he brought prosperity back to the region. However, in his creation of the Kingdom of Sicily, he also created enemies out of the Lombards, the Holy Roman Empire, the Byzantine Empire, and the pope. Even the Sicilian king Frederick II (r. 1198-1250), who became Holy Roman emperor in 1220, did not manage to resolve the various conflicts his kingdom had.

Since Frederick II was the Holy Roman emperor, he claimed his right over the communes of the Po Valley. He vowed to succeed where even Barbarossa had failed and bring imperial rule over the cities of northern Italy. Because of this threat, the Lombard League was revived, but it failed to defend its possessions. Frederick II defeated the League in 1237 at the Battle of Cortenuova. However, by demanding an unconditional surrender, he created even more resentment toward imperial rule. The following year, he failed to capture Brescia, along with Parma, in 1248. The Lombard League never surrendered, and in 1250, Emperor Frederick II died without fulfilling his vow.

In 1266, Charles I of Anjou, the brother of the French king, invaded Sicily and killed the last representatives of the Hauteville dynasty. When Charles transferred the capital from Sicily to Naples, he became very unpopular with his subjects. During the uprising of 1282, which is known as the Sicilian Vespers, Charles was expelled from the island, and the title of Sicilian king was given to Peter III of Aragon (r. 1275-1285; r. Sicily 1282-1285). Charles founded the Kingdom of Naples, which would remain a separate political entity until 1816 when the two kingdoms would merge and become known as the "Kingdom of the Two Sicilies." But the Aragonese rule of Sicily brought about a steady decline, as the island was now politically separated from France and the Holy Roman Empire. The Spanish Aragon dynasty would rule Sicily for centuries, and the island became closely tied to the Iberian Peninsula. But the king was rarely there; instead, he would send his viceroys to attend to Sicilian matters. This lack of direct attention slowly led to Sicily's decline.

The Venetian Republic

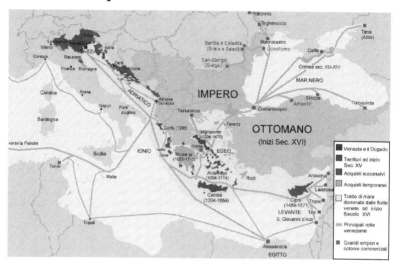

*Venetian expansionism during the 15th and 16th centuries
in contrast with the Ottoman Empire*

https://upload.wikimedia.org/wikipedia/commons/0/09/Repubblica_di_Venezia.png

Northeastern Italy had been a special case since the 5th century when the barbarian invasion of the peninsula took place. While retreating from the Vandal attackers, the people of these regions started creating communities in the lagoons of the Adriatic Sea. Venice was founded as early as 421, but it was not yet a city. During the next few centuries, more people arrived, trying to evade the Lombard invasion. These lagoons were nothing more than mudflats, little islets, and sandbanks. The first inhabited areas were at Torcello and Malamocco on the Lido. When the area took the shape of a city, a capital was founded on the Rialto Islands, which were elevated safely above water. This was a secure sanctuary, but since it was a swamp, it was also a challenge. The construction of buildings for housing required special architectural attention. Long wooden stakes were driven into the mud on top of which a platform of clay and wood planks was constructed. On these platforms, houses could be safely built. The Venetians didn't spare on the material, though. The houses and public buildings were built out of brick, stone, and even marble.

In the early years of its existence, Venice was a part of the Exarchate of Ravenna, and its local ruler was called a *dux* (later transformed into doge, equivalent to an English duke). As such, Venice was a part of the Byzantine Empire. In 726, the Venetians elected their first doge, who was their advocate for independence, but their efforts were unsuccessful. With the fall of the Exarchate of Ravenna in 751, Venice gained more autonomy, but it was still under the nominal rule of the Byzantine Empire. It is unknown when Venice gained full independence, but it was closely tied with the Byzantine Empire up until the fall of Constantinople. It seems that in the 12th century, the Byzantines already saw the Venetians as independent people, even though they helped defend the Byzantine possessions in southern Italy. Constantinople even brought forth a new edict in which Venetians were exempt from taxes on trade throughout the Byzantine Empire. Surely this edict wouldn't have been necessary if Venice was still under Byzantine rule. The constitution of Venice evolved between 1140 and 1160. Various institutions took away the power from the doges, and slowly, the city was turning into an oligarchic republic. In 1203, the Venetians even conspired and persuaded the Crusaders to attack Constantinople. Over time, they took more and more of the Byzantine territories, but they also maintained a professional relationship with their previous rulers. They even sent help to Constantinople in 1453 when the city finally fell to Ottoman rule, which marked the end of the Byzantine Empire.

Venice prospered because of trade and shipping. It didn't trade only with the Holy Roman and Byzantine Empires; it also spread its network throughout the whole Mediterranean world and beyond, later stepping into Asia and on the Silk Road. Their accumulated wealth allowed the Venetians to remain independent by buying various alliances whenever it was needed. They paid to prevent Venice from becoming a part of the Kingdom of Italy. They also financed the Lombard League's fight against Barbarossa, thus preserving their autonomy. However, many of their neighbors were jealous of their prosperity, so the republic had its share of enemies. Arabs, Slavs, Normans, and Ottomans all wanted the riches of Venice, or at least to include it in their growing empires. However, their enemies came and went, but there was one that lasted—Genoa. This city was a commercial enemy of Venice, and they battled each other for dominance in trade. The wars between the two Italian cities lasted from 1256 until 1381, with inconclusive results. Both cities suffered financially, and while Venice was able to regain its previous wealth, Genoa had no choice but to accept French rule to pay off its war debts. Genoa was in no condition to continue its fight with Venice over trade dominion in the Mediterranean.

After the Fourth Crusade and the sacking of Constantinople, Venice became a colonial power in the Mediterranean world. It already controlled the coasts of Dalmatia and Croatia, as it needed stone and timber from these areas, but in the 13th century, it spread its dominion over Crete, Corfu, Morea (14th century), and Cyprus and Salonika (15th century). In 1500, Venice took over Cephalonia. The Venetians' expansionism wasn't driven by their desire to rule but by their need for safe havens for their trading ships. The Venetians even had the Black Sea opened to their traders in the early 12th century. Venice was a world of ships, sailors, merchants, dockers, customs officers, and shipbuilders. They never grew plantations, and the only products of their own that they exported were closely related to shipbuilding. They exported refined timber, ropes, sails, etc. But since they had a great influx of raw materials, such as marble, precious metals and gems, silk, and peacock feathers, Venice became a great producer of luxury and decorative items.

The trade in Venice wasn't an individual occupation. It was heavily regulated and controlled by the government. The city organized convoys for its merchants, and the government built the ships. The shipyard of Venice, known as Arsenale (Arsenal), employed over 1,500 men during the 13th century. The workers, *arsenalotti*, were well paid and enjoyed many benefits, among them rewards in imported material goods. By the 16th century, the city developed a huge silk and glass industry, which was also regulated by the government. This and the trade across the Mediterranean world and into Asia made Venice the richest republic in the Christian world. The city offered political stability and personal freedom to its citizens, and in turn, there was never a revolt or a conspiracy against the government. However, when one mad doge tried to establish a monarchy in the 14th century, he was quickly discovered and executed.

The political system of Venice was complex, and even contemporaries of other Italian cities had trouble understanding it. But they all admitted that the system worked. The power wasn't concentrated in the hands of only one individual. It was dispersed among various councils and committees, who were elected by very complicated procedures. The doge was the elected head of the state, but he never ruled alone. He had a council of six individuals close to him (*Minor Consiglio*) and several ministers (*collegio*), who had executive powers. They were completely autonomous from the doge, and so was the Council of Ten (*Consiglio dei Dieci*), which was responsible for the security of the state. Venice also had a senate, which numbered approximately 200 men. They worked with the state's legislature. Beneath them was the Great Council (*Maggior Consiglio*), which had more than 2,000 participants, all from wealthy and powerful families. The members of the Great Council were the main elective body, and they cast their votes to choose a new doge, members of the *Minor Consiglio*, and various ministers.

Doges were not kings, and their power was very limited. Even though they lived lavishly in the palace or a house of their choosing, doges had to suffer some sacrifices. They were not allowed to trade or to accept gifts. They were also not allowed to own property outside of the Republic of Venice or even leave its borders without the permission of the councils. A doge was also not allowed to talk to foreign ambassadors on his own or to abdicate. If a doge had a son, he was not allowed to hold any office or vote, let alone dream of succeeding his father. Sons were also not allowed to marry a foreigner without the consideration and permission of both councils. Because a doge was elected for life, or as long as the people saw him fit for the role, they were often already old men who transferred their trade further down their family line.

Life in Venice was different from the rest of Italy, Europe, and the whole world. There, everyone was satisfied to play his or her role. Class differences existed, but the law was the same for noblemen and fishermen. The wealthy families didn't have their own set of rules by which they were judged, nor could they bribe the officials. Venetians believed in the good of the community, so that is how they acted. Everyone was allowed to trade and gather their fortunes under the keen eye of the state.

The nobles were often mocked in Europe because they didn't own estates or enjoy hunting in the forests, as the Republic of Venice couldn't offer them such luxuries. They didn't even have titles, and they would only use initials NH and ND in front of their names, which would designate them as *Nobil Homo* and *Nobil Donna* (Nobleman and Noble Lady). They were obliged to serve the public, and they even identified themselves with the state. The members of the noble families never worked as individuals to acquire personal wealth. They were an administrative body of the whole state, and personal wealth came only as a reward for their service. The cult of the individual was so weak that Venice doesn't even have any statues of noble people to commemorate their efforts.

Chapter 7 – Italy's Renaissance

The early Renaissance of Italy started with the city-states or the communes. There were no more foreign invasions, but that doesn't mean conflicts didn't occur. The rivalry between the communes was a reality, but so was the rivalry between different factions within the cities. There was no unity in Italy during the late medieval period, and there was none during the early Renaissance. This lack of unity and national identity created the perfect ground for disputes and conflicts. But it was probably the individuality each city experienced that greatly influenced their accumulation of wealth, splendor, artistic freedom, and beauty. The rivalry between the communities drove them to develop independently, and what remains as a standing witness of the Renaissance is the artistic identity of each Italian city. The constant competition in arts and science between the cities gave us some of the greatest Renaissance minds. Instead of inspiring armed conflict, the competition was sometimes healthy, and it brought forth various alliances, such as the renewed Lombard League.

But since the communes had no common ruler, let alone administration and bureaucracy, they were forced to expand at the expense of their weaker neighbors. Once a city's population grew, there was a constant need for new agricultural territories to sustain all the people. In Tuscany, Florence became the dominant power, and during the 14th century, it absorbed neighboring Prato, Arezzo, Pisa, and Siena. Other grand cities that were as powerful as Florence were Venice and Milan. These two cities controlled most of northern Italy. The conflicts between the cities continued until 1454 when the Peace of Lodi established the *Lega Italica* (Italian League). The members of this new league pledged they would defend each other if the necessity arose. The cities that signed were Milan, Florence, and Venice, but they were soon joined by Naples and the Papal States.

The era of peace and prosperity began, and individuals such as Leon Battista Alberti (1404–1472) started rising. Alberti was a typical "Renaissance man," an individual with multiple interests that he could engage with on a professional level. He was a priest, scholar of classical literature, poet, philosopher, comedian, and architect. He composed the first grammar of the Italian language and the first geography book in Europe since classical times. His best-known work is a survey of architecture in ten volumes. He was also an architect himself, and he built the beautiful churches of Sant'Andrea in Mantua and Santa Maria Novella in Florence. Alberti was just one such individual, as the Renaissance is known for producing many such men, such as Leonardo da Vinci, Michelangelo, and Galileo Galilei.

Another movement occurred during this period of Italy, and it often goes hand in hand with the Renaissance. Humanism, or the study of classical antiquity, revived interest in science. Even popes became patrons of the arts and sciences, as long as it glorified the religion. The individuals who were inspired to think beyond religion and beyond the known world were, at times, arrested and punished for their theories. One such individual was Galileo Galilei, who proposed that the earth is not the center of the universe and that it moves around the sun, not the other way around, which was how the Church teachings insisted. The Church strictly controlled what scientific discoveries were published, and many scientists were victims of the Inquisition.

Many famous people of the Renaissance, whether they were scientists, artists, philosophers, historians, etc., also served the public by accepting various positions in governmental offices. They felt the need to change the political system with their humanist ideas. They were administrators as well as scholars, and they modeled their political ideals on the example of the ancient Roman Republic. Coluccio Salutati was a chancellor of Florence, but he was also a bibliophile with an immense collection of classical texts. He was the first person to bring a Greek scholar from Constantinople to teach in Rome. There had been no Greek scholars in Italy since the fall of the Western Roman Empire. Another chancellor of Florence was Leonardo Bruni, who was a historian. Lorenzo Valla, a philosopher, historian, and humanist, was the secretary to the king of Naples.

Humanists revived the Italian love for freedom. They looked up to the ancient Romans but found inspiration in individuals such as Cicero or Virgil. They didn't look up to Caesar, Augustus, or any of the classical Roman dictators. It was as if the nation still remembered their unwillingness to be ruled by an individual. Their appreciation for classical antiquity went so far that Florentines claimed descendancy from Romulus himself, and they thought themselves to be the true Roman people. But their infatuation with the Roman Republic led to some unfortunate events. Many assassins considered themselves freedom fighters, similar to Brutus. Some of the members of the wealthy and famous Medici family were unnecessarily assassinated. While Venice was a more successful Renaissance republic, Florence harbored intellectuals and artists. Their painters were also innovators, and their scientists served the public. The largest brick dome in the world was constructed by Filippo Brunelleschi, an architect, artist, and the first modern engineer. It still covers the Santa Maria del Fiore (also known as the Florence Cathedral), and since the beginning of its construction in the 15th century, no one in the world managed to build a bigger or more grandiose brick dome.

Although it was a republic, Florence was a victim of factional conflicts. Venice was the only Italian city spared of such problems. In Florence, the powerful families constantly feuded, endangering the existence of the republic. In 1430, Florence finally succumbed to the Medicis, who became the ruling family. The Medicis were a Florentine family who earned their wealth through banking. Cosimo de' Medici used his wealth to bribe voters, and in 1434, he became the effective ruler of Florence. But the city was a republic, and Cosimo was only the first among equals, not a king. Therefore, the municipal council could always veto his political proposals.

During the Renaissance, the city-states often warred between themselves. Milan continuously attacked Florence, forcing the city to spend its resources on defense. On the other hand, Florence attacked other cities of Tuscany and often humiliated itself with its military incapability. The ruling Medici family even employed famous humanist inventors and engineers to help in the war effort, but even Leonardo da Vinci failed. He intended to divert the flow of the River Arno to leave Pisa without its water supply, but his miscalculations led to failure when the first storm knocked down his dam. Luckily, the Florentines were aware of their lack of military ingenuity, and they started paying mercenaries. The Church placed the blame for Florence's inability to defend itself on the low birth rate, which was the result of increased sodomy in the city (according to church officials). Even Niccolò Machiavelli, a famous Renaissance philosopher and senior official, was accused of sodomy.

The Medici family had connections everywhere in the known world. But their interest was mostly in Europe, and they produced two queens of France: Catherine and Marie de' Medici. The Medici family members became popes in Rome, as well as cardinals, archbishops, prominent diplomats, patrons of the arts, and republic officials. In 1527, the Medicis were exiled from Florence for their efforts to establish a monarchy. In 1531, with the help of Holy Roman Emperor Charles V, they took over the city again, and Pope Clement

VII (himself a Medici) made his cousin, Alessandro de' Medici, "Duke of Florentine Republic." This title became hereditary, and the Medicis now ruled as monarchs. Later, they were given the title of "Grand Duke of Tuscany," and the family ruled until 1737.

Italy had many republics during the Renaissance. Each city-state had its own government, as well as potential monarchs and powerful families who aspired to rule. Some republics even survived well into the 17th century, but then, they were absorbed by their more powerful neighbors or were simply extinguished, turning to monarchical rule. The 16th century saw Perugia and Bologna becoming a part of the Papal States. Milan oscillated between being a republic and a monarchy until its people had had enough and settled for a signorial government, which was run by a despot known as a signore.

During the late 16th century, the Italian republics gave way to monarchical rule. The rise of various princes and their courts took place, and the aristocratic values and lavishness returned. The rulers now chose their government officials instead of letting the electoral bodies do so. The rulers took upon themselves the role of patrons, and this role extended to the Church and pope to some extent. The days where the whole commune would invest in a palace and other official buildings were over. Artists now preferred to work in courts, and craftsmen and their group of workers were strictly employees of individuals rather than the government. This individual patronage allowed the arts to flourish, and some of the best Italian Renaissance painters were a result of this era. Raphael, Michelangelo, Titian, and Leonardo da Vinci were just a few who enjoyed the riches of various Italian courts. It wasn't unusual for an artist to move wherever his work would take him. It seems that only Venetian artists such as Tintoretto and Giovanni Bellini remained in their republic.

The Renaissance was not confined only to the Tuscan cities of Florence and Milan, nor was it unique for Venice. The Papal States and northern Italy were also big Renaissance consumers. At one point, the pope in Rome tried to take Florence's many humanists and artists by inviting them to be in his personal service. However, there was a huge cultural difference between central/north Italy and the south. In the south, Alfonso V of Aragon became the king of Naples and Sicily in 1442. He moved his court from Spain to Naples and adopted some of the Renaissance influences of his northern neighbors. However, he also brought the Spanish Gothic influence, and the two art forms blended. This style was short-lived, as the kingdom was again divided after his death in 1458. Naples was now under the cruel and incompetent rule of Ferdinand I, who neglected the cultural inheritance of the city.

Outside of Naples, southern Italy saw little to no Renaissance influence. Because the southern cities lacked independence and small courts that would be the patrons of the arts, they never managed to develop economically or culturally. In Apulia, the town of Lecce still bears the title of "Florence of the South," but its awakening occurred much later during the Baroque period (16th to 18th century). It seems that in the south, even the cities that prospered never renewed their interest for the classical period, and the Renaissance simply didn't hold any ground. Furthermore, many of the southern Italian cities today are more modern due to recent natural phenomena, which left them devastated during the early 20th century. Fortunately, the Baroque period didn't miss them, and today, they are some of the prettiest towns in Europe.

The lack of the Renaissance in the south can also be attributed to the constant conflicts between the ruling dynasties of Angevin and Aragon and the continuous feuds the monarchs had with their barons. Sicily never saw its Spanish rulers, and the aristocrats spent their money on buying titles from the kings and investing in various estates around the island. When the 17th century came, Sicily had a hundred little princedoms but only around one million inhabitants. Palermo was grandiose, but humanism passed it by, so it never housed intellectuals.

At the beginning of the Renaissance, Rome was in ruins. The pope moved to Avignon in the 13ᵗʰ century and left the city to fend for itself. The Rome of medieval times was forgotten, and its glorious classical heritage crumbled to dust. Even when the pope returned to Rome in 1377, what followed was the Western Schism and constant rivalry between various popes and antipopes. It wasn't until Pope Martin V (1417-1431) that the rebuilding of Rome could start. In just one century of tireless work by various popes, artists, and craftsmen, Rome became a city of palaces, fountains, refurbished aqueducts, paved streets, and many new churches. But popes of the Renaissance were also members of the wealthy and powerful families of Italy. They concerned themselves less with religion and more with the politics and rivalry of the ruling class. At the time, the popes more closely resembled the Renaissance princes than religious leaders. Corruption and opulence took over the papal residency, and some of them were even notorious for their enjoyment of earthly pleasures. Until the late 17ᵗʰ century, nepotism was a common occurrence in Rome, as each pope made sure his own family succeeded in important cardinal and papal offices.

The Counter-Reformation and the Wars of Religion

The decadent lives of the popes in Rome led to the Reformation in the 16ᵗʰ century, which started with the demands of Martin Luther, a German theologist. He observed how the disinterest of Renaissance popes led to a common practice of Catholic priests to gather personal wealth by selling plenary indulgences to whomever they wanted to buy it. The end result of the Reformation was the rise of Protestantism, which opposed the Catholic way of life, which was filled with pleasures, wealth, and sins. The Western Christian world found itself divided between Catholicism and Protestantism, and what followed was a series of religious-based wars throughout Europe. Even though they were based on religion, these were, in fact, about which faction would rise as the dominant one. Who would rule the Western world, the Catholics or Protestants? Such a turbulent period in Europe left its mark on Italy too. After all, it was (and still is) where the pope resided and where the conflict originated in the first place.

In 1545, the Council of Trent was formed, and its task was to counter the Reformation and restore the order within the Catholic Church. The council was to prohibit nepotism, prevent corruption, and deal with the clergy who continued to sell indulgences. It had many more issues to correct, but these were the main ones that occupied the mind of the first Counter-Reformist pope, Paul III. But the Council of Trent wasn't willing to please the Protestants and their demands. Instead, it sought to persuade them that the previously set values of Catholicism were the right ones. The Protestants demanded art be removed from sacred places, as they regarded it as distracting to the meaning of the text. They wanted people to be able to interpret the scripture and make their own conclusions. But popes believed that art improved and enriched the human vision of the divine.

This constant disagreement of Catholics and Protestants led to the creation of two not only religious but political streams of Europe. The wars that were fought throughout much of the 16th, 17th, and 18th centuries were about territory and power as much as about religion. This can be easily seen in the unusual alliances that were made. For example, Catholic France allied itself with the Protestants to fight another Catholic state, the Habsburg monarchy. Although Italy wasn't personally involved, its foreign rulers fought the Habsburg-Valois conflict for supremacy in Europe. The Habsburg Empire was divided between Spain and Austria. Spain continued to rule the Kingdoms of Naples and Sicily in the south, while the north and central territories of the Italian Peninsula now belonged to Austria. However, the Duchy of Milan belonged to both Spain and the Holy Roman Empire. This situation continued until the renewed conflicts in the early 18th century when the last member of the Spanish dynasty in southern Italy chose Philip of Anjou as his successor. The War of the Spanish Succession then started, even though the childless King Charles II of Spain chose his heir. These wars would greatly influence Italy, as the armies of both the Austrian and French kings occupied Sicily. At the end of the war in 1713, the Spanish claimant to the throne, Philip V (Philip of Anjou), was confirmed, although some of the Spanish territories in the American colonies were lost.

Austria hoped it would gain Sicily after the Treaty of Utrecht, which was one of the treaties that concluded the war, but a new claimant arrived: Victor Amadeus II, Duke of Savoy. Thus, Sicily again became a Franco-Italian possession, and Victor was crowned as the king of Sicily. But the aristocratic families of Sicily refused to accept the administrative and military changes Victor tried to implement. Instead of fighting the stubborn Sicilians, the new king decided to cede the island to Austria. However, Spain saw the opportunity to claim the island again, and they tried to invade it on two separate occasions, in 1720 and 1734. The second one succeeded, and the Bourbon dynasty continued to rule Sicily until 1860.

Sicily wasn't the only one suffering the consequences of the European religious wars. The ruling families in the north, such as the Medici and Farnese, died out by the 1730s. Florence and Parma were inherited by the family's female members, which then went to their foreign sons. Don Carlos, the son of the Farnese queen of Spain, became the next grand duke of Tuscany. But he wasn't satisfied with only having Tuscany, and while Europe was distracted by the War of the Polish Succession, he claimed the crown of Naples and Sicily. He soon became the king of Spain, where he was known as Charles III. He ruled until his death in 1788. The long chain of succession wars in Europe was finally coming to its end with the Treaty of Aix-la-Chapelle in 1748. However, Italy remained under foreign dynasties: the Bourbons in Parma and the south and the Habsburgs in Milan and Tuscany.

The Enlightenment of the French philosophers finally arrived in Italy, and the people learned that they should demand their monarch to be just, wise, and work for the profit of their territories instead of personal gain. The kings and queens accepted this new role of "enlightened despots," and they started investing in the country's agriculture, religion, education, and trade. Thus, Italy entered modern history as one of Europe's enlightened territories. It was ruled by foreigners, but it was still very much Italian at its core. The subjects of these new rulers remained the Lombards, Latins, Arabs, Greeks, and Jews—in other words, Italy was as diverse as ever.

Chapter 8 – The Modern History of Italy

Napoleonic Italy and the Unification of Italy

In France in 1793, the idea was born that the borders of the country should follow its natural borders, such as the Rhine, the Pyrenees, and the Alps. This would mean confiscating some of the territories of its neighbors, like the Austrian Netherlands. The Rhine was the most complicated border to acquire, as that was where the heart of the Austrian Empire began. After all, Austria was France's most powerful enemy in Europe. In 1796, it was decided that Napoleon Bonaparte (1769-1821) should lead the French armies in the war against the alliance between the Austrians and Piedmontese, which was, at the time, occupying Milan in Italy. If France was able to take these Italian territories from Austria, it could later use them as bargaining chips to move its border to the Rhine.

Napoleon was only twenty-six years old when he, with full confidence, led his army across the Alps. In several battles, such as the Battles of Lodi, Castiglione, Arcola, and Rivoli, he crushed the Austrian army, doing so in a couple of months. Bonaparte offered an alliance to Venice, but the republic wanted to remain neutral. This angered the French general, and he declared war on Venice. He kept his promise, and in the Treaty of Campoformio in 1797, the Venetian Republic was divided. Napoleon gave Eastern Venetia to Austria, while the western parts were incorporated into Lombardy, which itself was now part of the French Republic and the Italian Kingdom, which were all under the rule of the French government.

But with this modern French rule came new oppressive taxes on the Italians. The French came up with laws by which they could tax the foreigners for the liberation performed by the French troops. They were also allowed to confiscate any art pieces they found valuable, and the foreigners had no right to revolt. The French government failed to understand that this would make them unpopular with the people. They firmly believed in their propaganda, and they even printed newspapers in which they would communicate to Italians that they should be grateful for their freedom, pay for it, and learn how to preserve it. But the freedom came with a high price, even before the taxes were implemented. In just the first day of the "liberation," Milan was robbed by the French Army, and the estimated value of the taken items was above twenty million francs. Two types of sacking took place in the Italian cities. The first one would occur on the day of the battle, where soldiers would confiscate whatever they pleased from the enemy or from the people they were supposedly freeing. The other type of sacking was official and legal. The army would capture the city's bank and munition, then demand food and clothing for their soldiers. Government officials would come directly from Paris just to collect the captured money and art. Most of the Italian valuable art pieces are still in French museums today, The Horses of Saint Mark and the Venetian Lion of Saint Mark used to be, but luckily, both of these Venetian treasures were returned in 1815.

After realizing how successful Bonaparte was in capturing all of these territories, France gave up on the idea of natural borders and promoted a new idea: sister republics. Once France became an empire, these sister republics were turned into satellite states.

Napoleon spent eighteen months in Italy before he got tired of it and decided to search for a fight with England over some other territory. At the time, the French and the British were fighting over the overseas colonies. Bonaparte left for Egypt, leaving Italy to be cared for by the French Directory (the governing body of the French First Republic). The Directory was very aggressive, and it continued the military efforts in Italy. They drove Duke Ferdinand IV out of Naples and Duke Ferdinando III out of the Duchy of Tuscany. By 1799, France had conquered the whole Italian Peninsula. But France's enemies soon arrived in Italy, and Naples was taken by the British, while the north was torn between the Austrians and Russians. The French Directory managed to lose all of its Italian possessions within just a few months. The only city that was still under their control was Genoa.

When Bonaparte returned from Egypt in 1799, he was determined to overthrow the Directory and become the first consul of France. Once he achieved this, he sent General André Masséna to Italy with the task of defending Genoa from the Austrians. But Napoleon wasn't resting in Paris. He organized a new army, which he led across the Alps, intending to retrieve Lombardy. The decisive battle was fought in 1800 at the village of Marengo in Piedmont. The French almost lost the battle against the Austrians, but the French reinforcements arrived just in time to save the day. This battle was crucial for Napoleon, not only in taking Italy but also for his career. If he had lost the Battle of Marengo, he would have lost his consulship and would have returned to Paris disgraced. Tuscany was renamed the Kingdom of Etruria, and it was given to Ferdinand, the Bourbon Duke of Parma, as Napoleon planned to annex the Duchy of Parma. Farther north, he annexed Piedmont and installed the Italian Republic under the French governorship, with himself as its first president. The Italian Republic also included Novara, Verona, and papal Romagna.

Very soon, Napoleon Bonaparte proclaimed himself the emperor. He believed he was adept at ruling just like Charlemagne, and he wanted to make France the heart and soul of the newly installed Holy Roman Empire. Napoleon was crowned in 1804 by Pope Pius VII in Notre-Dame in Paris. The papacy was glad an empire was back in control, and Napoleon promised Pope Pius he would be the sovereign of Rome. However, he made sure the pope understood that he, Napoleon, was his emperor. In 1805, Bonaparte established the Kingdom of Italy and took its crown. This kingdom included the territories of the previous Italian Republic, Eastern Venetia, the Papal Marches (the Papal States under local rulers who answered to the pope), and Trentino. The far north of Italy was annexed to France. But Napoleon wasn't satisfied, and he soon added Liguria, Etruria, Parma, and Piacenza to the kingdom. Finally, he took the rest of the Papal States when Pope Pius VII was imprisoned in France, and it remained a part of France until the collapse of the French Empire.

When Napoleon took Naples in 1805, he installed his brother Joseph as its king. However, Joseph was recalled after only two years as he needed to take the rule of Spain. Naples was then given to Marshal Joachim Murat, Napoleon's brother-in-law. By 1810, the whole Italian Peninsula was ruled by Napoleon, and he divided it into three blocs: Imperial, Italian, and Neapolitan. Sicily and the surrounding islands were in the hands of the British, and this was the only Italian territory where Napoleon had no access.

Although Italy was part of the French Empire, it didn't benefit from it. Napoleon used Italy as a source of tax revenue, and he continued to confiscate its art. Because France was at war with all of the greatest European forces—Austrians, British, and Russians—Italy's foreign trade came to a halt. The constant conflicts of the Napoleonic Wars also decimated the inhabitants of the peninsula, and the loss of life didn't just come from the wars. People who stood up to the French rule over Italy were executed, no matter if they were men or women. However, some good came out of Napoleon's rule in Italy.

The laws were changed in such a way that they allowed even wider religious freedoms, and many cities had to knock down the walls that confined the Jewish to ghettoes. Divorce was introduced, as well as a new set of laws that regulated inheritance. Old roads were renewed, and new ones were built. The Napoleonic fiscal and institutional reforms in Italy were the foundations of its modern state. However, Napoleon was hated in Italy, as he ended all hope of the peninsula's independence. In their hatred toward him, the people united without even realizing that slowly, but surely, they were growing into one nation.

When Napoleon's empire fell in 1814, the European powers gathered in Vienna to repair the borders that France had constantly tampered with. They tried to restore the Italian states that had existed in 1789, but they soon realized this was impossible since it could cause further conflicts. Italy's three Napoleonic regions were reformed into nine states (it had eleven in 1789). The Italians acquired a greater love for their country during the Napoleonic Wars, and they lobbied to gain independence or at least some level of autonomy, but once more, they became the subjects of Austria. Austria's presence in the Italian Peninsula was meant to act as a shield against the possible revival of a French invasion. The Austrian king also received the newly founded Kingdom of Lombardy-Venetia, while his brother Ferdinand III took over the Grand Duchy of Tuscany. Marie Louise, his daughter, received Parma, while the Bourbons were given Lucca. The papacy got back its Papal States, and the Habsburgs ruled Modena. The Bourbons were again the kings of Naples.

Italy was once more under foreign rule, and the people saw this period as the dark ages of the Italian peninsula. "Repression" and "reaction" were words that could be heard everywhere, as Italy's foreign rulers were regarded as oppressors. The pope's restoration to temporal power was certainly a return to the Dark Ages, as the religious freedoms brought by the French were suppressed. The popes also dismantled any industrial changes the French had brought to the Papal States, such as street lights, railways, and vaccinations, which they claimed were works of the devil.

The Italians, although not yet a united nation, were ashamed of what their peninsula had become. The people fell to lethargy, as they saw no exit from the oppressive rule of foreigners. They were unaccustomed to fighting and were depressed due to the poverty and chaos that awaited them after each war. Their country was robbed of its precious art, and foreigners often mocked Italians as people who had nothing to be proud of. Classical Rome was still lingering in the peninsula in the form of ruins, and although it attracted visitors, Italy itself had nothing to offer anymore. After learning their history, new generations were ashamed of their heritage, of their incompetent ancestors who never fought for freedom, who did nothing to resist the foreign invasions. A new type of artist emerged during this period, one who sought heroes of which to be proud of. They celebrated Barbarossa's defeat by the Lombard League as a national achievement. Some artists, who were humiliated of being Italian, went so far as to make up their own heroes and attribute them to the peninsula. Others drew inspiration from mythological scenes, claiming they were real Italian achievements. One such is a scene that originates from the 16th century when thirteen Italian knights challenged thirteen French kings in a duel, and they won. But there was no Italy in the 16th century, and the myth, although attractive, remains a lie.

This ever-present sense of humiliation for being born in the Italian Peninsula and the need for pride and heroes of the past slowly started spreading the seeds of national unity. Even though each part of the peninsula fought separately, the Italians finally gained some inspiration to fight for their freedom. At first, the fight was on a very small scale. The people, who were inspired by Spain, which had just introduced a constitution, demanded their rulers implement laws that would protect them. But the Austrian rulers were ruthless, and they would rather suppress any small uprising than consider a change in their government. When the citizens of the north realized they were under the same oppressive yolk as the people in the south, their shared troubles united them, even though they were under different rulers. At first, the young dreamers of a united nation traveled from north to south, inspiring the people by shouting, "Viva la Italia!" Soon, this shout became a battle cry as the revolution began to take hold of the whole peninsula. Following the revolutionary trends of Europe, Italy rose up in 1848. The first place to do so was Sicily, and the people managed to overthrow their Bourbon ruler. However, this freedom lasted for only sixteen months.

One by one, other states followed, and revolutionary outbreaks in Tuscany, Lombardy, Venice, and the Papal States occurred. Pope Pius IX was even chased away from Rome, where the patriots of Italy, led by Giuseppe Garibaldi, founded the new Roman Republic. Unfortunately, the French saw an opportunity to profit from Italy, and they allied themselves with the pope. By June 1849, the pope was back in Rome with temporal power in his hands once more. In the rest of Italy, the Austrians moved to restore order and reinstall the rulers who had been expelled by the revolutionaries. The revolution had been completely crushed a year after it had started. But the dream of unification persisted.

This dream culminated ten years later, in 1859, with the start of the Second Italian War of Independence. This time, the French leader, Napoleon III, emerged as an ally of Sardinia, as he was willing to expel the Austrians from the Italian Peninsula. The French and Sardinians expelled the Austrians from southern and central Italy. The northern volunteer army, which was led again by Giuseppe Garibaldi, was victorious at the Battles of San Fermo and Varese. A treaty was signed the same year, in which Austria kept Venice, and Lombardy was annexed to Sardinia.

The people were not satisfied with this outcome. The wisdom of the Sardinian leaders was demonstrated in their choice to continue the fight, but this time, they did so with diplomacy rather than war. The result was the formation of the Kingdom of Italy in 1861. Even though it seemed that another war was unlikely, the diplomatic approach didn't work out for all the included parties—Italy, France, and Austria. Peace was achieved, but everyone was unsatisfied with its results. In 1866, the Third Italian War for Independence broke out when the Kingdom of Italy saw an opportunity to capture Venice by allying itself with Austria's newest enemy: Prussia. Austrian Emperor Franz Josef I was unable to lead the war on two fronts, and he was forced to cede Venice to Italy through an agreement with Napoleon III.

Rome was still under the protection of France, and even though Napoleon III allied himself with the Kingdom of Italy in the fight against Austria, he refused to cede Rome. However, once the Franco-Prussian War broke out in 1870, he was forced to recall his troops from Italy, including the ones defending the Eternal City. This was Italy's opportunity to capture Rome and add it to its kingdom. But Pope Pius IX disagreed, and even though he had only around sixty men defending the city walls, he mounted a resistance. On October 2nd, the soldiers of the Kingdom of Italy entered Rome and annexed it, together with Latium. The pope locked himself in the Vatican and refused to leave. Even though nobody prevented him from leaving, he declared himself a prisoner of the Vatican in defiance to Italian unification.

Italy was finally unified, but governmental problems arose. The main problem was how to govern the southern territories, which had their representatives in Piedmont, where the first administrators, bureaucrats, and state officials were elected. The south was often accused of being corrupt and barbaric, and Piedmont needed to evaluate the socioeconomic situation there to conclude the governmental model by which it would be ruled. The conclusion was that since Italy was a kingdom that was governed by a parliament, the southern regions would have to be ruled by that same parliament since they were too barbaric and untrustworthy. The first king of the newly unified Italy was Victor Emmanuel II (r. 1861-1878), who was previously the king of Sardinia. Today, he is regarded as a national hero, and there are many statues depicting him all over Italy. He chose Turin as the new capital of his kingdom, but Rome would take that title after it was conquered. Italy remained a kingdom until after the Second World War, in 1946, which was when it became a democratic republic.

Italy and the World Wars

The Kingdom of Italy at its greatest extent in 1943

https://en.wikipedia.org/wiki/File:Kingdom_of_Italy_1943.png

The third generation after Italian unification had many reasons to detest their king. King Victor Emmanuel III, the grandson of Victor Emmanuel II and his namesake, made a series of decisions between 1915 and 1946 that proved fatal to his country and, in the end, to his own rule. He joined both world wars, even though his people wanted to stay neutral, and in 1922, he refused to declare martial law, which would have prevented Benito Mussolini from rising to power. Finally, in 1940, he refused to abdicate in favor of his son, and he pushed the people of Italy to vote for the republic.

When World War I started in 1914, Italy was part of the Triple Alliance with Germany and Austria, which secured them defense from any other world power that might attack. Italy entered this alliance because of possible French attacks, and in turn, it promised it would help Germany against possible future attacks from France or Russia. But Italy was in a dilemma about which side to choose when conflict broke out after the assassination of Archduke Franz Ferdinand, the heir to the Austro-Hungarian throne. The Italian people wanted to remain neutral and not meddle in what would soon rise to become World War I. The following year, Austria offered Italy some of its territories just so it could remain neutral. However, two Italian politicians thought they would gain even more territories if they joined the war. These men were Antonio Salandra, the prime minister, and Sidney Sonnino, the minister of foreign affairs. However, they were in the minority, and to push Italy into the war, they needed their king's help.

Together, they bargained with Britain, France, and Russia, and in a secret meeting, they signed the Treaty of London, an alliance in which Italy promised they would declare war on Austria and Germany. In return, Italy was promised the territories of Trieste and Trentino, Gorizia, Istria, South Tyrol, parts of Dalmatia and Albania, and some of the Adriatic islands. When war was finally declared in 1916, the Italians believed they were fighting for the unredeemed lands of the Italian Peninsula. It wasn't until 1917 that they found out the details of the Treaty of London and learned they were fighting for foreign territories. The people were appalled by this knowledge, as they had no desire to be the conquerors. They saw themselves as liberators and revolutionists and wanted to remain such. A strong party was formed that opposed the war, and it included the nationalists, the socialists, and the pope. Even though the opposition easily outnumbered the pro-war party, the people of Italy fell victim to propaganda machinery.

In the end, King Victor Emmanuel III acknowledged that Italy went to war even though the majority of its population and its parliament opposed it. But it didn't matter since Italy was already at war, and Benito Mussolini worked tirelessly to suppress any anti-war protests that might occur. Mussolini was a member of the Italian Socialist Party, but he was expelled from it in 1914 for his pro-war ideas, and he founded his own political party, the Fasces of Revolutionary Action. There were rumors that he was financed by the British secret service and the French, as they both wanted Italy to intervene in the war on their side. He published his newspaper *Il Popolo d'Italia* ("The People of Italy"), in which he promoted his pro-war ideas. He even served in World War I in 1916, but due to serious wounds he received on the war front, he was allowed to return to Rome, where he started his political career. Upon his return, he founded a new political party, the National Fascist Party. It was then revealed that he was paid 100 pounds each week for his services by the British to keep the pro-war mood in Italy.

World War I ended in 1918, with great losses on each side. Italy lost one-third of its population, but it claimed that the Great War made its people more patriotic and happier to fight for its country. However, this seems to be very far from the truth. Written evidence was found of soldiers' testimonies that talk about how they tried to avoid going to war. They ate cigarettes to make themselves sick, and they even put tobacco under their arms to insulate heat, which would make them appear malarious. Many Italian officers testified that the soldiers serving under them surrendered easily, and they, at times, gladly threw their weapons down when facing the enemy. The soldiers from southern Italy could barely understand their northern compatriots, and there was no love between them. The Italian soldiers spat on the nationalist flag, as the government made them fight for faraway countries they never even heard of. Modern anthropologists collected stories of various Italian villagers who fought in the world wars, and the result was astonishing. Nobody wanted to fight, and no great sense of nationalism was felt among the people, except among those who were already members of the Italian Nationalist Association.

Although Italy was on the winning side of the war, it didn't get the territories it was promised by the 1915 Treaty of London. When the United States joined the war in 1917, it insisted that after the war, new borders should be drawn by recognizable national lines. Italy protested, and in the end, it gained all of the promised territories except Dalmatia. Mussolini was one of the Italian leaders who demanded the territories in the Balkans, and his fascist movement united all the people who weren't satisfied with the outcome of the war, no matter if they were war veterans, futurists, nationalists, or socialists. When the elections came in 1921, the National Fascist Party got under 2 percent of votes. This is because, at the time, their politics were unorganized, and they had no political identity. The Socialists refused to enter a coalition with Giovanni Giolitti, the Italian prime minister. Instead, they threatened a revolution to establish a republic. When Giolitti approached Mussolini and the Fascists, they refused the coalition as well and instead joined the Socialists. The Socialists were already the biggest political party in Italy, and by accepting the Fascists, they opened the way for Benito Mussolini to recruit people from their ranks. In just three years, the Fascists became powerful enough to start a government.

At this point, Mussolini started talking about the fascist revolution. His ideology was a combination of traditionalism, futurism, conservatism, and revolution. Fascism drew from the past but somehow managed to look to the future. Mussolini dressed his followers in black shirts, and soon, they became a paramilitary organization that would often beat their opponents into submission. Because fascism is so contradictory, it is today still very hard to find the intellectual coherence in it. In the 1930s, Mussolini started parading his fascist followers. There were more uniforms on the streets, more speeches from their leader and prominent members, more censorship, and plenty of shouting. One could hear "Patria and gloria!" ("Fatherland and glory") being shouted in the streets. Mussolini was welcomed everywhere he went with chants of "Duce! Duce!" ("Leader! leader!"), with his followers becoming more and more entranced by the movement. This sudden transformation of fascism from a political party, which originally had barely any support, to a massive movement of people can be connected with the rise of Adolf Hitler in Germany.

With each passing year, Mussolini changed his ideology bit by bit. Although the Fascists at first tolerated Jews and found them to be no threat to Italian nationalism, Mussolini later on claimed he was always an anti-Semite. However, there is evidence of several Jews being close members of Mussolini's cabinet. Even his first lover was found to be Jewish. In 1938, Mussolini accepted the Nazi philosophy of race superiority. He even integrated it into his movement, claiming it was a political and evolutionary dogma. People such as Arabs, Blacks, and even Slavs were seen as inferior, as the movement believed that only fair-haired, blue-eyed northerners were capable of ruling. This was a strange belief to take hold in Italy since blue eyes and fair hair were (and still are) rare features. Nevertheless, Mussolini claimed Jews had to be expelled from the peninsula to preserve the purity of the Italian race.

During the first year of the Second World War (1939–1945), Italy remained neutral. Perhaps this hesitation was due to France, Italy's neighbor, being too mighty. Mussolini was aware the Italian Army was weak, disorganized, and undisciplined. He politically embraced

Germany, but he refused to enter the war until France was occupied. Once the French government fled in front of the Nazi invasion, Mussolini stepped in and joined Germany in its occupation. He probably hoped to gain some of the French territories by defeating the enemy, which was already on its knees. On September 27th, 1940, Japan, Italy, and Germany signed the pact that established the Axis Powers.

Inspired by Germany's victory in France, Mussolini immediately made demands for territories in Europe, Africa, and the Middle East, but Hitler replied that the British needed to be defeated before any such plans were made. The Nazis persuaded the Italians to use their Libyan army, which was stationed there since Mussolini's attempt to conquer Africa in 1938. Mussolini was supposed to capture the Suez Canal and defeat the British in Egypt. However, he was more interested in the fight in Europe, and he decided to attack Greece. In October 1940, he moved his troops from Albania into Greece, where the numerically inferior enemy army made the Italians retreat. Mussolini then changed his mind and ordered an attack in Egypt. But there, the results were even more disastrous. The Italian Army, under the leadership of Rodolfo Graziani, who would later become the minister of defense, was utterly defeated by the British. Over 250,000 Italians were part of the Egyptian offensive, and 36,000 British troops managed to defeat them in a series of engagements. Hitler even offered to send German tanks with the Italian Army to Egypt, but Mussolini refused help, as he wanted his army to achieve pure glory. In the end, Hitler had to finish the conflict in Africa with his own army. And in Greece, where the Italian Army had failed, Germany had to go to their rescue. Because Germany had to go out of its way to help its Italian ally, the invasion of Russia was postponed. Maybe this was what contributed to their defeat on the Eastern Front. But what is known is that the failures of Italy placed this country in a subordinate position within the Axis pact.

The main task Italians had at this point in the war was to garrison the Balkans while the Germans and the Japanese did all the fighting. In southeastern Europe, the Italians proved to be very bloodthirsty. They ruthlessly persecuted Yugoslavian guerilla fighters (Partisans), and many civilians suffered, as Italian soldiers accused them of harboring the enemy. In Ljubljana alone, the Italian troops shot over a thousand hostages and 8,000 civilians. Over 35,000 people were deported to concentration camps.

In July 1943, the Anglo-American forces landed on Italy's mainland. They spent the next twenty months progressing slowly toward the north, through the Apennines, where they relentlessly fought the Germans. At this point, the Italian Grand Council voted to return the command of the country to its rightful king, Victor Emmanuel III. The king was never really deposed but rather shared the power over the country with Benito Mussolini. He ultimately allowed Italy's entrance into the war by being passive; in fact, the king permitted Mussolini to enter the Second World War in June of 1940. After three years of war, Victor Emmanuel realized his mistake when the Allied forces approached Salerno. Finally, he accepted the Anglo-American terms of an armistice. But even then, the king was unsure, and he betrayed his new allies at the first sign of German occupation. His ineptitude to mount a defense led to the Nazis taking the north of the peninsula and progressing south as far as Naples. The king feared for his life, and he ran away to Brindisi, abandoning all of his obligations to the country and the war. In the Balkans, the Italian soldiers who fought on the side of the Axis were now arrested by the Germans since Italy officially sided with the Allies. Nearly one million Italians in the Balkans were arrested, but only 6,000 of them tried to fight their way to freedom. They were all killed by the Nazis.

When Victor Emmanuel first took the command of the Italian military forces, Benito Mussolini was arrested and imprisoned in an Alpine ski resort. The Germans had the perfect opportunity to save their ally, and they did so, installing him as the king of Salo (the Italian

Social Republic), a new fascist state in the north of Italy. There, the remnants of the Italian Fascists and Nationalists gathered together, and they proudly fought for their new republic. But Mussolini was demoralized, and he had no real power. He couldn't do anything since he was a puppet ruler under the iron heel of Nazi Germany. However, he managed to provoke his fellow Italians who opposed him, and they created the Italian partisans to resist the new Italian Social Republic. As a result, a civil war broke out in the north of the Italian Peninsula. In April 1945, only nineteen months into its existence, the Italian Social Republic was crushed. Mussolini tried to escape while dressed as a German officer, with piles of money in his pockets. He was arrested at Lake Como and was soon shot by the Italian Communists.

Without Mussolini and with king Emmanuel having fled, Italy hit its lowest point during World War Two. The recently united nation was torn between Germany, Britain, and American rule. At the end of the war, the British and Americans couldn't allow Victor Emmanuel to return, as he was a betrayer who had been tainted by the politics of Nazi Germany. Instead, they forced him to turn the power over to his son, Umberto I. However, Emmanuel refused to abdicate and even insisted on staying in Italy. This made him incredibly unpopular with the people, who claimed that they were against Italy joining the war in the first place. When a referendum on whether to continue the monarchy was held in 1946, the king won 10,700,000 votes, but that wasn't enough, as 12,700,000 people voted for the abolition of the monarchy. Crown Prince Umberto concluded that his throne was not worthy of the bloodshed that would follow if he insisted on preserving the monarchy. He accepted the elections and went into exile in Lisbon, Portugal. The male heirs of the Italian royal family were not permitted to return to Italy until 2002. Even then, they were forced to promise they would renounce their claim to the throne if they wanted to visit the country.

Conclusion

After World War II, Italy started its slow and painful journey to a better tomorrow. Unfortunately, the nation was again divided, with some regions demanding separation. To appease them, the Italian Republic government approved the autonomy of Sicily, Sardinia, Val d'Aosta, and Trentino-Alto Adige. They were joined by Friuli-Venezia Giulia in 1963. In the north, there was a large concentration of people who refused to admit they were Italians and instead spoke French, German, or one of the Slavic languages. The clash of the Christian Democrats and the Italian Communists occurred in the mainland, as the first didn't want to be ruled by the so-called incapable communist administrators from Florence, Perugia, and Bologna. More demands for autonomy were raised, while those regions who were granted autonomy earlier cried out because their freedom was restricted by the communist government.

Finally, in the 1970s, the government divided Italy into the regions we know today. During the 1990s, the regions were given autonomous power over matters of tourism, transport, welfare, and other sectors. In 2008, there was a proposal to let the regions collect their own taxes, which would decentralize the country. It seemed that Italy was about to accept diversity and regionalism. But the path to this "fiscal federalism" is long, and the government needs to pass many more laws to allow the regions to be completely fiscally independent.

Today, Italy is divided into twenty regions. Each is subdivided into hundreds of provinces and around 8,000 municipalities. This led to the duplication of government positions, and many efforts were made to abolish the provinces. However, the Italians would not allow it. They claimed that the provinces were their national heritage, and they wouldn't let them go easily. While the local government today is mainly in the domain of the municipality, wider issues are dealt with at the regional level. Even though Italy is officially united, each region prides itself as if it was a different nation. Although Italians love their countrymen, animosity between the regions is not unheard of; however, today, it is reduced to a level of friendly competition. Italian diversity has gravitated toward unification since classical times, yet the people remain divided by their cultural and regional differences. What is the future of Italy? It remains as unpredictable as its past, and only time can tell.

Here's another book by Captivating History that you might like

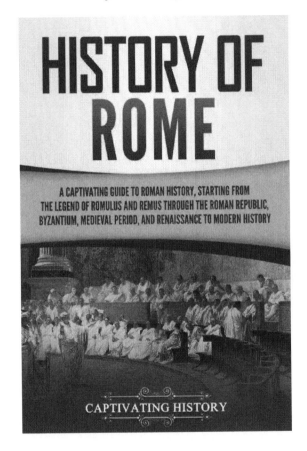

Free Bonus from Captivating History
(Available for a Limited time)

Hi History Lovers!

Now you have a chance to join our exclusive history list so you can get your first history ebook for free as well as discounts and a potential to get more history books for free! Simply visit the link below to join.

Captivatinghistory.com/ebook

Also, make sure to follow us on Facebook, Twitter and Youtube by searching for Captivating History.

References

Appianus, McGing, B. C., Appianus, & Appianus. (2019). *Roman History*. Cambridge, MA: Harvard University Press.

Badoglio, P. (1976). *Italy in the Second World War: Memories and Documents*. Westport, CT: Greenwood Press.

Bagnall, N. (2008). *The Punic Wars: Rome, Carthage and the Struggle for the Mediterranean*. London: Vintage Digital.

Bondanella, P. (1973). *Machiavelli and the Art of Renaissance History*. Detroit: Wayne State University Press.

Bradley, G. J., Isayev, E., & Riva, C. (2007). *Ancient Italy: Regions without Boundaries*. Exeter, UK: University of Exeter Press.

Bradley, H. (1910). *The Goths: From the Earliest Times to the End of the Gothic Dominion in Spain*. London: F. Fisher Unwin.

Daim, F., Dillon, J. N., & Smart, D. (2019). *History and Culture of Byzantium*. Leiden; Boston: Brill.

Eristavi, N. (2010). *From Celtic, Etruscan and Roman Hands: The Po River Valley and Modena (Mutina)*. München: GRIN Verlag.

Fell, R. A. (2013). *Etruria and Rome*. Cambridge: Cambridge University Press.

Gross, N. L. (1922). *The Papal States: Their Rise and Fall.* St. Francis (Wis.): St. Francis Seminary.

Hazlitt, W. C. (1966). *The Venetian Republic; Its Rise, Its Growth, and Its Fall 421-1797.* New York: AMS Press.

Kulikowski, M. (2007). *Rome's Gothic Wars from the Third Century to Alaric.* New York: Cambridge University Press.

Laven, P. (1971). *Renaissance Italy: 1464-1534.* London: Methuen.

MacNamara, E. (1991). *The Etruscans.* Cambridge, MA: Harvard University Press.

Mango, C. (2004). *The Oxford History of Byzantium.* Oxford: Oxford University Press.

Mikaberidze, A. (2020). *The Napoleonic Wars: A Global History.* New York: Oxford University Press.

Moser, M. E. (1989). *The "Southern Villanovan" Culture of Campania.* Ann Arbor: University Microfilms International.

Mussolini, B., Klibansky, R., & Lobb, F. (2000). *The Mussolini Memoirs 1942-1943: With Documents Relating to the Period.* London: Phoenix.

Prodi, P. (1987). *The Papal Prince: One Body and Two Souls: The Papal Monarchy in Early Modern Europe.* Cambridge: Cambridge University Press.

Rothenberg, G. E., & Keegan, J. (2006). *The Napoleonic Wars.* Washington, D.C.: Smithsonian Books.

Stierlin, H., & Stierlin, A. (2004). *The Roman Empire: From the Etruscans to the Decline of the Roman Empire.* Köln: Taschen.

Strachan, H. (2003). *The First World War.* Oxford: Oxford Univ. Press.

Wilson, P. H. (2017). *The Holy Roman Empire: A Thousand Years of Europe's History.* London: Penguin Books.

Printed in Great Britain
by Amazon

64406291R00070